"... DO ALL TO THE GLORY OF GOD"
1 Corinthians 10:31

Basic Lesson Series—Volume 5

DO ALL TO THE GLORY OF GOD

"Exercise thyself unto godliness"
1 Timothy 4:7

WATCHMAN NEE

Christian Fellowship Publishers, Inc.
New York

Available from the Publishers at:

11515 Allecingie Parkway
Richmond, Virginia 23235

Basic Lessons—Volume 5

CONTENTS

BASIC LESSONS
ON
PRACTICAL CHRISTIAN LIVING

Burdened with the need of a firm foundation for the Christian life, brother Watchman Nee gave a series of basic lessons on practical Christian living during the training session for workers held in Kuling, Foochow, China in 1948. He expressed the hope that these essential lessons might be faithfully learned by God's people, thereby laying a good foundation for the building up of the Body of Christ.

These messages on practical Christian living have now been translated from the Chinese language and will be published in a series of six books, bearing the various titles of: (1) *A Living Sacrifice;* (2) *The Good Confession;* (3) *Assembling Together;* (4) *Not I, But Christ;* (5) *Do All to the Glory of God;* and (6) *Love One Another.*

"Exercise thyself unto godliness" (I Tim. 4:7), is the exhortation of the apostle Paul. May our hearts be so exercised by God's Word as to give the Holy Spirit opportunity to perfect the new creation.

All quotations of the Scriptures, unless otherwise indicated, are from the American Standard Version of the Bible (1901).

MARRIAGE

To be a good Christian, one needs to deal faithfully with all one's basic problems. If there is a moral issue in any of these basic areas, whether it be family or profession or whatever, other problems will later on crop up. One undealt difficulty is strong enough to hinder growth and deter one from walking uprightly.

In this lesson we will consider the problem of marriage. New believers especially need to know what the Word of the Lord says about this problem. Let us, then, look at the problem from various directions.

Sex Consciousness Not Sinful

People are conscious of sex just as they are conscious of hunger. If hunger is a natural, physical demand, then sex is also a natural requirement of the body. For a person to feel hungry is natural and it is not a sin. But if he steals food, then it is sinful. It is something unnatural. Likewise, the consciousness of sex is natural and is not reckoned as sin. Only if one uses an improper way to satisfy his desire does he fall into sin.

1

Sex consciousness is God-given. Marriage was ordained and created by God. It was instituted before, not after, the fall of man. It happened before Genesis 3. As a matter of fact, God introduced it in Genesis 2. Hence, sex consciousness existed before, not after, sin entered into the world. It is important to know that there is no sin in being sex conscious. Sin is not primarily involved, for the very presence of this consciousness was created by God.

In my thirty years of trusting and serving the Lord, I have been in contact with not a small number of young brothers and sisters. Some people are not easily disturbed, whereas others, I find, are greatly troubled by unnecessary accusations of their consciences. Their consciences are troubled by uncalled-for accusations because they do not know God's mind nor are they clear about God's Word. They think they have sinned in being sex conscious. Some brothers have even gone to the extreme of doubting God's work in them since they are yet aware of sex. To treat sex as sinful is a heathen idea. As it is not sinful to feel hungry, likewise the need for sex is not at all sinful. It is but a natural consciousness.

The Lord tells us through His apostle, "Let marriage be had in honor among all" (Heb. 13:4). It is not only something to be honored but is holy as well. God considers sex both holy and natural.

Dr. F. B. Meyer wrote many good books in which he stressed building up Christians. He said that only a dirty mind would consider sex as dirty. I think this is well said. Man injects dirty thoughts into sex because he himself is dirty. To the clean everything is clean. To the unclean, nothing is clean. His thinking will always be dirty. But marriage itself is clean. The sex relationship which God has ordained is holy, clean, and undefiled.

Paul shows us that in later times there will arise doctrines of demons, among which is "forbidding to marry" (1 Tim. 4:3). This particular doctrine of demons seems like a seeking for holiness. In G. H. Pember's writings, he points out clearly how people forbid marriage in the pursuit of holiness. They think that this will make them holy. But in 1 Timothy, it is explicitly stated that forbidding to marry is a doctrine of demons. God has never forbidden marriage.

May no believer be accused in his conscience because of heathen teaching. Sex consciousness is natural; it is not sinful. The problem does not lie in the presence of such consciousness but, rather, in changing it into sin. The presence is not sinful but the way of treating such consciousness may make it sinful.

Three Basic Reasons for Marriage

1. FOR MUTUAL HELP

Marriage is ordained by God. "It is not good that the man should be alone" (Gen. 2:18), God says. All things created by God are good. On the first day of creation, God saw the light and said it was good. On every day except the second, God proclaimed it was good. (The second day was an exception because then the firmament, Satan's dwelling place, was created.) But on the sixth day, after God created man, He said, "It is not good that the man should be alone" (Gen. 2:18). This was not to suggest that the man had not been well created; it only meant that it was not good because only half of man was created.

So, God made a helpmeet for man. Eve was also made on the sixth day and was brought by God to Adam. She was made for the express purpose of marriage.

The word "helpmeet" means "meet to help"; that is, she must first answer or correspond to Adam before she can be of help to him.

When God created man, He created them ma and female. It seems as if He first created half of man and then made the other half so that there would be one whole man. Only after the two halves were joined together was man completed. Then God pronounced that "It was very good" (Gen. 1:31). First of all, it needs to be pointed out that marriage was initiated by God, not by man. Further, it did not originate *after* the fall of man, but *before* man ever sinned. Man did not sin on the first day of his creation, but he was married that very first day. After God created Eve, on the same day He gave her to Adam. So marriage is indeed instituted by God.

In Genesis 2 God's creation is recorded; in John 2 the wedding in Cana during which the Lord Jesus turned water into wine is recorded. This latter incident shows us that the Lord Jesus not only allowed marriage but also approved it. He was present at the wedding and helped to make it a success. God initiated marriage and the Lord Jesus approved it.

God's purpose is that the husband should have a wife to help. That is why the wife is called "helpmeet." God wants the husband and the wife to live together, fellowshiping, and helping each other.

2. For Prevention of Fornication

In the Old Testament, before sin came into the world, God had already instituted marriage. But now, in these New Testament days, sin has already come in. So Paul shows us in 1 Corinthians 7 that, because of the entrance of sin, marriage not only is not prohibited but, rather, has become a necessity.

In order to prevent fornication, Paul tells us that each man should have his own wife and each woman her own husband. He does not condemn sex consciousness as sin; instead he suggests that marriage can prevent the sin of fornication.

Paul says, "Make not provision for the flesh" (Rom. 13:14). This is a most marvelous thing. For example: Suppose a person is caught in the sin of pride. Paul cannot say to him, "Because you are prone to be proud, I will let you be proud at home lest you be proud everywhere. If you have one place to be proud, you will not be proud other places." For God to say that would be making provision for the flesh. God never makes such a provision. If a person likes to steal, you do not say to him, "Since you like to steal, I will allow you to steal only the things which belong to brother so-and-so, so as you will not steal elsewhere." Instead you will tell him, "I will not allow you to steal, not any place." Stealing is entirely sinful; therefore no provision can be made for it. Pride is an unqualified sin; hence no provision can be made for it. But sex is not categorically sinful; so each man should have his own wife and each woman her own husband. Sex consciousness is not sin, or else Paul's words would be making provision for the flesh. We know, however, that the apostle does not make provision for the flesh; hence sex is not a sin. Let us remember that God has not made provision for the flesh by permitting marriage. Marriage is holy, and it is instituted by none other than God Himself.

After sin came into the world, marriage became necessary to prevent fornication. In no way, though, is this to be considered as making provision for the flesh.

When Paul spoke on marriage, he said in 1 Corinthians 7:4, "The wife hath not power over her own body, but the husband: and likewise also the husband hath not power over his own body, but the wife." His teaching on this is very clear. He says in verse 5, "except it be by consent for a season, that ye may give yourselves unto prayer, and may be together again, that Satan tempt you not because of your incontinency." The husband and the wife should generally not be separated in order that fornication be prevented. Thus God ordained marriage and decreed that the husband and wife should stay together.

"It is better to marry than to burn" (1 Cor. 7:9). Paul writes strongly here. Those who have a compelling desire for marriage and who burn should be married. He does not reprimand them for their strong sensation, as if it were sinful, nor does he make provision for the flesh. He only states that if people have a strong feeling toward marriage it is better for them to marry than to burn. The Word of God is clear on the matter. Sex consciousness is not sin. Even a strong sexual urge is not sin. But God does prescribe marriage for such people. They should not refrain from marriage because to do so might cause them to fall into sin.

3. FOR RECEIVING GRACE TOGETHER

In speaking to husbands and wives, Peter says, "as being also joint-heirs of the grace of life" (1 Pet. 3:7). In other words, God delights in having the husband and the wife serve Him together. He looks for Aquila and Priscilla to serve Him, for Peter and his wife as well as Jude and his wife to serve Him.

New believers should know that there are three basic reasons for Christian marriage: first, for mutual help;

6

second, for prevention of sin; and third, for receiving grace together before God. Marriage does not involve just one Christian, but two Christians together in the presence of God. Not merely one person receives grace, but two are joint-heirs of the grace of life.

The Problem of Virginity

The Bible is really wonderful, for it shows us on the one hand that sex is not sinful and marriage is initiated and ordained by God to prevent sin, and yet it suggests on the other hand that it is well for those who do not have a strong sexual urge and who have no great need to satisfy that desire to keep their virginity.

1. PURPOSE OF VIRGINITY

Virginity is not holier than marriage, but virgins have the advantage of being able to be careful for the things of the Lord with their entire physical strength.

Paul shows us that the married have three hardships. First, marriage is a bondage. He says, "Art thou bound unto a wife?" (1 Cor. 7:27). Once married, many things need to be attended to. Second, the married shall have tribulation. "Yet such shall have tribulation in the flesh" (v. 28). Naturally, after marriage, the tribulation in the flesh will be increased so that you cannot serve the Lord without distraction. Third, the married is careful for the things of the world (vv. 32–34). Such carefulness, as the Lord Jesus says in Matthew 13, can easily hinder the wheat from bearing fruit, for the cares of this life choke the wheat and prevent it from yielding fruit. So, marriage has its hardships: bondage, trouble, and care.

Paul does not speak to workers only but to all brothers

and sisters. He who keeps his virginity is spared many hardships. Paul gives no command for virginity, but he does incline toward it. Actually, he is only revealing facts. It is well for brothers and sisters to be married, for they will avoid the danger of sinning; but they will be bound, suffer more tribulation in the flesh, and have more cares of life.

2. WHOM VIRGINITY IS FOR

Paul tells us who can keep their virginity.

GIFTED FROM GOD

He who has the gift from God can keep his virginity. Virginity is a gift. "Howbeit each man hath his own gift from God, one after this manner, and another after that" (1 Cor. 7:7). Some need to be married, for they have received the gift of marriage. Without this gift, no one can be married. As keeping virginity is God's gift, so is marriage the gift of God.

Concerning the virgin, the first condition is that though there is sex consciousness, there is no sexual compulsion in the person. Some people have a strong sexual urge, while others have only the consciousness but not the compulsion for it. The latter alone may keep their virginity.

STEADFAST IN HEART

"But if any one think that he behaves unseemly to his virginity, if he be beyond the flower of his age, and so it must be, let him do what he will, he does not sin: let them marry. But he who stands firm in his heart, having no need, but has authority over his own will, and has judged this in his heart to keep his own virginity, he does well" (vv. 36–37 Darby). In the Greek, the word points to virginity, not to daughter as in some translations. If someone thinks he has not treated himself properly toward his virginity, he should marry. But he who is inclined toward keeping his virginity and is steadfast and determined may do so.

ENVIRONMENTAL DIFFICULTY

Those who may keep their virginity are those who, first, have no sexual compulsion but only sex consciousness; second, are determined in their hearts before the Lord to keep their virginity; and third, have no environmental problem, "no need" (v. 37). Some people have environmental troubles, hence virginity is not easily arranged. They may have family pressures or other difficulties which make it impossible for them to keep their virginity. Therefore, virginity is possible only when the environment is favorable.

3. THE RELATIONSHIP OF VIRGINITY TO THE
   KINGDOM OF THE HEAVENS AND TO RAPTURE

He who is able to keep his virginity really has much to gain before God. I think Matthew 19 shows us clearly that it is easier for a virgin to enter into the kingdom of the heavens. We have to acknowledge the distinct relationship between virginity and the kingdom in the word, "made themselves eunuchs for the kingdom of heaven's sake" (v. 12). We dare not define what the relationship is, but we can truly say that virginity has its advantage in entering the kingdom. Because of this, the Lord mentions how some make themselves eunuchs for the kingdom of heaven's sake.

There is also the passage in Revelation 14 where we see the one hundred and forty-four thousand who are the

9

firstfruits to God and to the Lamb. They are virgins (v. 4) and they follow the Lamb whithersoever He goes. Thus we see virginity is especially related to rapture.

According to the teaching of the Bible, marriage is holy and not to marry is also holy. Marriage is good and not to marry is better. Not to marry gives one more freedom to serve the Lord. This matter must be clearly presented to brothers and sisters so that they may make their choice before God.

The Other Party in the Marriage

The Lord has laid down definite conditions as to whom one can or cannot marry. The Bible indicates clearly that the marriage of God's people should be limited among themselves. In other words, if there is to be a marriage, the opposite party must be sought among God's own people. One may not marry someone outside the scope of God's people.

1. OLD TESTAMENT TEACHING

The Old Testament contains sufficient charges to confirm that we should not marry outside God's people.

THE CHARGE IN DEUTERONOMY

Neither shalt thou make marriages with them; thy daughter thou shalt not give unto his son, nor his daughter shalt thou take unto thy son. For he will turn away thy son from following me, that they may serve other gods: so will the anger of Jehovah be kindled against you, and he will destroy thee quickly.

Deut. 7:3–4

The people of Israel were not allowed to marry the

Canaanites. New brothers and sisters should see that, according to Old Testament teaching, the other party in marriage must be one in the Lord. Do not seek a wife or a husband outside the faith. The greatest problem lies in the possibility that the other person may lead you away from the Lord to serve other gods. It is very easy for the wife to follow her husband and for the husband to follow his wife in worshiping idols. Since they are married, it is simple to worship the other's idols.

THE WARNING OF JOSHUA

Else if ye do at all go back, and cleave unto the remnant of these nations, even these that remain among you, and make marriages with them, and go in unto them, and they to you; know for a certainty that Jehovah your God will no more drive these nations from out of your sight; but they shall be a snare and a trap unto you, and a scourge in your sides, and thorns in your eyes, until ye perish from off this good land which Jehovah your God hath given you.

Josh. 23:12–13

Joshua also warned against the people of the land, for these would become a snare and a trap. Foreign wives and husbands would be thorns to them and would ensnare them till they were destroyed.

THE RETURN OF NEHEMIAH

When Nehemiah returned to the land of Judah after his visit to the land of his captivity, he found that many of the children of Israel could not speak the Jews' language as the result of mixed marriages. So he contended with them and made them separate completely from the foreign women (see Neh. 13:23–27). The trouble with marrying a Gentile woman is that sooner or later the children will follow their mother and fail to serve God with you. If you marry a Gentile, with your own eyes you will see your children fall into the world. This, indeed, creates a difficult situation.

THE TIME OF MALACHI

Judah hath dealt treacherously, and an abomination is committed in Israel and in Jerusalem; for Judah hath profaned the holiness of Jehovah which he loveth, and hath married the daughter of a foreign god.

Mal. 2:11

Marrying the daughter of a Gentile is, in the sight of God, profanity against His holiness. Therefore, Christian marriage is limited as to whom the other person may be. Marriage must be between believers.

THE FAILURE OF SOLOMON

Solomon was the wisest of kings, yet he fell into idolatry through marrying foreign women.

2. NEW TESTAMENT TEACHING

In the New Testament, Paul writes clearly as to whom the other party in a marriage may be.

THE WORD TO WIDOWS

A wife is bound for so long time as her husband liveth; but if the husband be dead, she is free to be married to whom she will; only in the Lord.

1 Cor. 7:39

BE NOT UNEQUALLY YOKED

Paul tells us whom we may marry in this famous

passage, "Be not unequally yoked with unbelievers" (2 Cor. 6:14). Though this word is not directed exclusively to marriage, it does include marriage. For a believer and an unbeliever to work together in order to arrive at one goal is like putting opposite types of animals together under one yoke to till the ground. This is something God forbids. God does not allow the believer to bear the same yoke with the unbeliever. In the Old Testament it is specifically charged, "Thou shalt not plow with an ox and an ass together" (Deut. 22:10). The ox is slow, while the ass is fast. One wants to go one way; the other wants to go another way. One goes heavenward; the other goes to the world. One seeks for spiritual blessing; the other for earthly abundance. One pulls in one direction while the other pulls in another direction. This is an impossible situation. Such a yoke cannot endure.

The most serious yoke of all is marriage. Of three examples—partnership in business, an enterprise jointly undertaken, or marriage—the last constitutes the heaviest yoke. It is really difficult to bear the responsibility of the family together. The ideal second person in the marriage must be a brother or a sister. Do not carelessly choose an unbeliever. If you do, you will immediately get into great trouble. The believer pulls one way, while the other migrates toward the world. One seeks for heavenly gifts, but the other looks for earthly wealth. The difference between the two is tremendous. Because of this, the Bible commands us to marry those in the Lord.

If Married to an Unsaved Person

Here is a problem. Suppose a brother is already married to an unbelieving wife, or a sister is already married to an unbelieving husband. What should he or she do in such a situation? This is different from the preceding problem, for that refers to those not yet married but seeking a life partner. The problem here, though, is that one is already married to an unbelieving wife or husband. What, then, should be done?

1. IF HE LEAVES, LET HIM

1 Corinthians 7:12–13 and 15 answer this question. The Lord Jesus in the Gospels predicts that there will be troubles in the family. If one believes thoroughly in the Lord, there will be conflict at home. Luke records what the Lord says, "For there shall be from henceforth five in one house divided, three against two, and two against three" (Lk. 12:52). Such division is caused by some of the family believing in the Lord. If an unbelieving husband wants to depart because of his wife's faith, saying, "I do not want you any more since you have believed in the Lord," what should his wife do? The Word of the Lord is clear. "Let him depart" (1 Cor 7:15). So it is also with an unbelieving wife and a believing husband. If she insists on leaving, let her go.

But one thing must be clear: let him or her take the initiative; the believer must not initiate the separation. It is not the believer who wants to leave, but the unbeliever who so wishes. It is the latter who is discontent, thinking that there is no future because the former has believed in the Lord.

2. IF HE STAYS, THE LORD WILL SAVE HIM

If the unbelieving wife or husband is content to dwell with the believing one, Paul says, let him or her not leave his wife or her husband. God has called us to peace. The unbelieving is sanctified in the believing. It may be that the unbelieving wife or husband will be saved. If there is a separation, it must come from the unbeliever, not from the believer. But if the unbeliever does not ask to leave, we trust the Lord will save that soul. It seems quite easy that the Lord should save such ones. Let us, therefore, stand on this ground in respect to the matter.

If Engaged to an Unsaved Person

Sometimes brothers or sisters have already been engaged to an unbeliever. What, then, should they do?

1. THE UNBELIEVER MAY BREAK THE ENGAGEMENT

It is clear that the Lord does not want us to marry unbelievers. But if a person is already engaged, it is a different matter. It is best if the unbelieving fiancé or fiancée voluntarily asks to break the contract, for they are only engaged, not yet married. Should the Lord open the way so that the unbeliever offers to break the engagement because of the believer's faith, it is well. Otherwise, there will be some difficulties.

2. THE BELIEVER MAY NOT CARELESSLY ANNUL THE CONTRACT*

Such a voluntary offer does not always happen. Even though the opposite party realizes that you have come to

* To be sure, in Western culture very few people would hold to such a strict application of this aspect of engagement as presented by the author in the following three paragraphs. Yet the principle is good and should be carefully considered by all believers. Vows that are taken should not be so easily broken.—*Translator*

believe in the Lord, he or she may still hold on to the engagement. At that time, you need to remember that in becoming engaged, you have given the other party a contract, a promise to him or her before God. A Christian should not annul such a contract carelessly, for a contract is sacred in the sight of God. You, as well as the opposite party, may suggest an annulment. Such a suggestion does not need to be initiated only by the other party as is the case with a married couple. This is only an engagement, so you may initiate the suggestion. However, if the opposite party insists on your fulfilling your contract, you will have to fulfill it. When the word of a Christian is already given, it must be enacted; it must not be destroyed. Because God keeps His word, we have salvation; otherwise, there would be no salvation. Thus we can only negotiate, but we cannot unilaterally destroy the contract. If the opposite party does not give consent, the contract must be carried out.

"Who shall dwell in thy holy hill? . . . He that sweareth to his own hurt, and changeth not" (Ps. 15:1, 4). We may illustrate this with the story of the Gibeonites (Josh. 9). They craftily planned against the people of Israel and deceived the latter with dry moldy bread, old patched shoes, and worn garments. They said they came from a far country and got Joshua to make peace with them to let them live. Later it was found out that they actually were neighbors. But, because the covenant had already been made, God would not allow Israel to kill them. Instead they were made hewers of wood and drawers of water for all the congregation. This indicates how seriously the keeping of a covenant is regarded in the Bible. If the other party wishes to annul the covenant, then I am free to forfeit it. But if he insists on its terms, I must fulfill it. This covenant with the Gibeonites produced a serious consequence. Saul in his zeal slaughtered the Gibeonites (see 2 Sam. 21). Because of this, rain was withheld from heaven and there was famine in the land. David asked the Gibeonites what he should do for them in order to make atonement. The Gibeonites demanded that seven of the sons of Saul be hanged on the tree. David had to comply with this demand. God will not allow us to carelessly destroy a covenant. We must, therefore, learn to keep any covenant which we have made.

Hence, in this matter of marriage, if the unbeliever is unwilling to be separated, then the believer must not force the separation. The contract must be fulfilled by getting married.

3. BEFORE MARRIAGE, THE BELIEVER SHOULD NEGOTIATE CONDITIONS

But one thing the believer can do, and that is, before the marriage certain conditions should be negotiated. First, the believer must get the unbelieving party to consent to his or her serving the Lord. There should be no hiding or pretension. The flag must be fully unfurled. As a Christian, he or she must be given freedom to serve the Lord with no interference. Second, when children are born into the family, they must be brought up according to the teaching of the Lord. The other party may not believe in the Lord, but the children must be nurtured in the admonition of the Lord. These two things need to be settled before marriage, or else there will be difficulties. For a believer to marry or be given in marriage to an unbeliever is undoubtedly a loss. We wish to lessen the loss and minimize the difficulties. We must ask for freedom to serve the Lord and to bring our children to the Lord. We are Christians. We will not go into the world but will follow after the Lord. If the opposite party consents to our conditions, it is fine. If not, let him abrogate the engagement.

The Problem of Divorce

The Bible is explicit about divorce; divorce is allowed on one condition only. The nations of the world permit many and various reasons for divorce, but the Bible permits only one. The one and only condition for divorce is adultery; there is none else. Mental cruelty or physical absence does not constitute Scriptural ground for divorce. The Lord Jesus states clearly, both in Matthew 19 and Luke 16, that divorce is permitted in case of adultery.

1. MARRIAGE NOT TO BE BROKEN

You may ask, why is divorce permitted when there has been adultery? Because what God has joined together, man should not separate (Matt. 19:6). In other words, the husband and the wife are one in the sight of God. Divorce is a declaration that this oneness has been violated. Adultery has destroyed it, for the one who commits adultery has destroyed the oneness of the husband and the wife.

2. DIVORCE PERMITTED AFTER ONENESS LOST

Why is divorce allowed in the case of adultery? Because the oneness has already been broken. When a husband or wife commits the sin of adultery the oneness between the husband and the wife is destroyed; hence the mate is free. Originally there was oneness, and it must be kept. But once this oneness is forfeited, the marriage partner is freed.

18

Adultery, therefore, is the sole condition for divorce. If a husband commits adultery, his wife may leave if she wants to. Likewise, the husband may leave if the wife commits adultery. The church should not hinder this. The other partner may have a divorce and may remarry.

Divorce is merely a declaration. It declares that the oneness is broken. Thus the offended partner may marry again.

What, then, is divorce? It is the breaking of oneness. This actually happens at the time of adultery, not at the time of divorce. Divorce is but the procedure that pronounces that the oneness no longer exists. As marriage announces the presence of this oneness, so divorce pronounces the end of it. Hence, divorce is permitted after adultery. Divorce without adultery as its cause, however, is entirely a different matter. Any other grounds for divorce causes adultery as a result.

Let us recognize that marriage is oneness. The two people are no longer two but have become one flesh. Adultery destroys this oneness and divorce declares the breaking of it. What therefore God has joined together, let not man put asunder.

The Problem of Widows

The Bible allows those who have lost their husbands or wives to marry again.

Marriage ends at death. In the resurrection, the marriage relationship no longer exists, for in the resurrection men neither marry nor are given in marriage. Marriage is a thing of this world. Angels do not marry, nor will men in the resurrection. Marriage belongs to this age, not to the age to come. Consequently, marriage ends with death.

After the death of one's life-partner, the living one may remarry or may, for the sake of past affection, remain unmarried.

Let us notice the teaching of Romans 7. Here we see that in a sense every Christian is a remarried person. Through the death and resurrection of Christ, we have remarried. The Word of God shows that "the woman that hath a husband is bound by law to the husband while he liveth; but if the husband die, she is discharged from the law of the husband. So then if, while the husband liveth, she be joined to another man, she shall be called an adulteress" (vv. 2–3). Romans 7 teaches that if the law had not died, we could not belong to Christ, for that would make us adulteresses since we were married to the law. But through Christ we are made dead to the law. We can choose Christ today without being adulteresses. We are now married to Christ, for we have died to the law. Likewise, in the church today there should not be the concept of forbidding widows to marry again. Such a concept is heathen in origin.

Of course, it is well for a widow to abide as she is, living on the same principle as those who keep their virginity. "But I say to the unmarried and to widows, It is good for them if they abide even as I" (1 Cor. 7:8). To live alone as a virgin in order to serve the Lord is absolutely right. But not to remarry because of criticism and a worldly concept is not right.

"I desire therefore that the younger widows marry" (1 Tim. 5:14), so says Paul to Timothy. These young widows should be married just as widowers remarry. The question is whether one has such a need both physiologically and psychologically. Some feel lonesome. This is a psychological problem. Some have family needs. It is right, therefore, for either the brother who has lost his wife or the sister who has lost her husband to marry again. Christians ought not to criticize people on this account.

The Question of Sin

1. WHAT SIN IS

Sex outside of the marriage relationship is sin. God in His Word recognizes that sex is right, sex consciousness is right, even sexual intercourse is right. To be conscious of sex is not only right but is also holy. Only, it must be limited to the marriage relationship. If it is within the bounds of marriage, it is both right and holy. New believers need to be shown that there is no sin in sex consciousness or sexual need. It is an holy thing. But God does put a restriction around the sexual act: it is right only in marriage, in the oneness of the husband and the wife. Any sex consciousness or sexual action outside of marriage is sinful. Do you see what sin is? Sex becomes sin when it is active outside marriage. Why? Because sex outside marriage breaks the oneness of the husband and the wife. It is sinful not because of sex itself but because it destroys oneness. Sex itself is not sinful. This we must see clearly before God.

2. CONSENT OF THE WILL CONSTITUTES SIN

The Lord Jesus in Matthew 5 says, "Every one that looketh on a woman to lust after her hath committed adultery with her already in his heart" (v. 28). The word "look" here involves the will. It is not just seeing a woman but looking at a woman. Seeing is passive, but looking is active. It is not the stirring of lust at seeing a woman, but the looking at a woman because of lusting after her. The lust comes first, and then the looking. So, this look is the second look, not the first look. The second look is actually the third step. First one sees a woman, then lust is stirred in his heart, and lastly he takes a second look, lusting after her. Everybody sees women. Some people, though, have no control over themselves. They start to have lustful thoughts, and they also accept these evil thoughts that Satan injects. They turn around and look the second time. This is sin.

In other words, what Matthew 5 means is that he who looks at a woman with lustful thoughts in his mind has already committed adultery in his heart. It is not the first look that is here considered. A person may see a woman on the street accidentally, but he has not sinned if he resists the lustful thoughts which Satan tries to inject into his mind. Only when he turns and looks the second time does he really sin. Remember, therefore, sex consciousness is not sin, but the consent of the will is sin, for the will consents to sex outside marriage. He who consents has already destroyed the oneness of marriage in his will. It is sin to destroy this oneness in action; it is equally sinful before God to destroy this oneness in will.

MATING

And Jehovah God said, It is not good that the man should be alone; I will make him a help meet for him.

Gen. 2:18

Introduction

When God created man, He made him in two halves. With the exception of those few who have been given the gift to remain single, everyone should marry. Most Bible teachers believe that when a child of God chooses a mate, it is but the result of an effort to find the other half. To choose a mate simply means to find the other half God has created for you so that the two halves may become one whole. Older brothers and sisters should instruct younger ones to seek the other half. Such searching is for the purpose of making one whole. Halves are ineffective if they remain halves. Only those who find the corresponding half are complete. However, to put two halves together at random may cause much trouble. We believe that what God has joined together no man can separate. So the young need to find the one to whom God has joined them.

The marriages of young brothers and sisters greatly affect the church. If there are problems in the marriages, these will soon become church problems. So, young people must be led aright in this matter.

Concerning the matter of choosing one's mate, we hope young brothers and sisters will be open and unprejudiced before God about this. Deal with the matter objectively, not subjectively. To be too subjective easily makes one's heart and head too hot to be able to see clearly or to see everything. Learn to remain calm and objective. Deliberate everything carefully before God. Do not leap into anything on the impulse of over-heated emotion. A Christian can jump into marriage but he cannot jump out of it. We Christians cannot behave like people in the world who easily marry and easily divorce. We cannot jump out. Therefore, before you jump in, consider carefully.

I will mention some basic conditions for mating, going from the outward to the inward. I do so with the hope that young brothers and sisters will calmly consider them one by one before God.

Natural Attraction

The marriage between Jacob and Rachel was more easily concluded than that of Jacob and Leah, for the former was based on natural affection. We must not despise natural attraction. In choosing a mate, not just any brother or sister will do. To be brothers and sisters involves no question of attraction, but to be joined in matrimony involves consideration of many factors. Attraction is one of these factors.

Dr. Bevan of the Christian and Missionary Alliance, a greatly used servant of the Lord, said that when the Lord makes you a brother or a sister to all the brothers and sisters, the question of attraction is not involved; but when He causes you to marry a brother or a sister, there is bound to be the matter of attraction. New believers need to know that there must be natural attraction. As a matter of fact, this hardly needs to be taught, for they know it already!

When you are choosing a mate, you must love to be with the other person and enjoy his or her company. You should not merely endure the presence of the opposite one but should find delight in being together. If you do not enjoy each other's company, you should not be married, for a basic condition is lacking. Furthermore, such delight in, or enjoyment of, the company of the other party must not be of a temporary nature; rather, it should be of long duration. You should sense that even after thirty or fifty years you will still love to be together.

Health

1. Love Can Overcome

It is possible that weakness of body in the other party can be overcome by great love. Indeed, sometimes a person gets married out of a great love desire to minister to the physical weakness of the opposite party. There was once a brother in England who married a sister because the latter was blind. There are many other similar instances in church history. Because the love was great, it overcame the physical weakness.

2. The Ordinary Situation

We must notice, however, that we cannot expect to find

such great love in everyone. Generally speaking, a weak body tends to imperil the success of a marriage. If one is often sick, the other party will have to sacrifice much, and this will naturally affect the prosperity of the marriage.

The one who must receive help due to physical weakness does have a greater possibility of being either selfish or overly sensitive. A selfish person can only take but not give, only receive but not spend. The person weak of body may, out of selfishness, take it for granted that he or she must be helped. As time goes on, this selfish spirit becomes so evident that the opposite party begins to feel disgusted and looks down on the weak one. Or, if the receiver is not a selfish person, he or she may become very sensitive. This too is quite a problem. As the weak one continually receives help from the husband or the wife, he or she may be overwhelmed by the thought that the opposite party has to make such a great sacrifice. This makes the days very difficult for the recipient of such grace.

Now let us consider the one who serves. That one either may willingly sacrifice or may feel that it has become too much. When the flesh is weak, a person's patience may be exhausted by giving. Human patience is not without its limit. When patience runs out, family trouble begins. Sometimes, however, it is not a running out of patience but a downright unwillingness to sacrifice.

Because of these things, we wish to point out that although physical health is not in itself too big a problem, it can become a difficulty in the future of the family. Although at the time of marriage it may not constitute a problem, afterward it may be another matter.

For example, I know a husband who is seriously ill. His wife has to work outside in order to support the family. So she works during the day and takes care of the house at night. Such a situation can continue for a short period of time but certainly not for too long. The wife may work for one or two months but not forever. Such an arrangement should not be overly prolonged.

I believe for a marriage to be successful both the man and the woman should be comparatively healthy. Neither of them should be seriously ill, or else in a time of special trial the burden may become unbearable.

Heredity

Marriage must be coolly considered from a long-term point of view. Therefore the matter of heredity needs to be taken into account. One should take into consideration the health of the progenitor as well as that of the individual.

1. EFFECT ON THE NEXT GENERATION

Heredity is not only a matter for scientific study but is also considered in the Bible. God's law is: "For I Jehovah thy God am a jealous God, visiting the iniquity of the fathers upon the children, upon the third and upon the fourth generation of them that hate me, and showing lovingkindness unto thousands of them that love me and keep my commandments" (Ex. 20:5-6). Many live dissipated and lawless lives in their youth because their fathers or grandfathers before them sowed the wind (Hos. 8:7a). He who sows by a wind lives wantonly. Such a person may be forgiven, saved, and receive new life. But, though qualified to be saved, he may not be fit to marry. The Lord forgives his sin and causes him to be saved, but his child may not be saved so easily. Evil seed can be transmitted to the next generation, but the new birth cannot be. It is possible to plant the seed of sin, but it is impossible to propagate regeneration.

All too frequently the next generation becomes more sinful and less lawful. This causes much sorrow to the parents. Sometimes people wonder why such a spiritual person has such an awful child? Why does such a good sister have a profligate girl? It may be because the law of the body passes to the second and the third generations. What has been sown to the wind shall be reaped in the whirlwind. One reaps what he has sown. Such sowing and reaping may bring into one's own family a most difficult child and into the church a sinner who finds it hard to repent. It creates quite a problem.

2. GOD'S MERCY

However, those who do have a hereditary problem and are already married should seek God's mercy. They should ask to be delivered from the governmental hand of God. The consequences of heredity belong under God's governmental hand too; His ordering is involved. So, we should ask that His hand pass over and that the natural consequences be averted.

Family Background

There is a Western proverb which says, "I marry her, not her family." This is not strictly true, for when a girl marries, her family usually comes along.

1. FAMILY INFLUENCE

A person is more or less influenced by his or her family. In considering marriage, one should pay attention to the moral standard of the other person's family. Are they of noble ideals? How strict a standard do they maintain? What is the attitude of the men toward women and vice versa? By looking into questions such as these, one may safely deduce what one's future home will be like.

A boy or a girl who has been under his or her family's education for twenty years or so will unconsciously carry the old family way into the new home. This will happen even if he or she is dissatisfied with the old family. Sooner or later the old ways will crop up. I dare not say this will happen ten out of ten times, but I dare say it will occur seven or eight out of ten times. Although the old family ways may not appear all at once, they gradually will seep in. So young people need to know that to safeguard the success of their marriage they should notice these things and carefully weigh them one by one.

If the father of a family treated his children with excessive sternness, you may expect that the son or daughter from that family will probably not be too affectionate. But if the family is peaceful and the parents are full of love, you will see that the children from that family are usually gentle and easily able to get along with others. A child who comes from a family in which both the father and the mother are strict will generally be introverted because for twenty years or so his feelings have not been toward his father or mother but toward himself or herself. To choose an undemonstrative husband from such a family is all right, but certainly one should not expect him to be a warm and outgoing husband. The same applies in the choice of a wife. In seven or eight out of ten cases, the family situation is reproduced in the second generation.

2. THE MOTHER

"If one desires to marry a daughter, look at her mother." This saying is more or less true. By looking at the way the mother treats the father, you will know how the daughter will treat you. She has watched this for over twenty years and this is surely what she has learned. Having seen her mother's daily way with her father for years, it would be most difficult for her not to treat you in the same way. Likewise, by looking at a father, you will know how the son will treat his wife.

For example, a headstrong person may for a time exhibit great gentleness in conversation. But if he comes from a family of strong character, sooner or later he will reveal his stubbornness. If he is from a family where there is restraint and no shouting, he will usually be courteous and careful in his words and deeds. He at least knows that it is wrong to quarrel. For him to scold and fight is like asking him to climb over a high mountain. But if a person comes from a home where fighting and scolding are daily portions, the story is different. Though he or she may show great politeness today, this behavior is undependable; it is only temporarily put on. Some day all that he or she has learned at home will break forth. It will be easy for him or for her to scold and to fight.

For this reason, it is well for a man to look into the woman's family background before marrying her, and likewise the woman into the man's. In perhaps seven out of ten cases, the children are like their parents. Do you like the family? If you do, you can more or less expect your future home to be of a similar kind. If you do not approve, you should not expect your mate to be an exception. It is not easy to be exceptional.

3. THE WHOLE FAMILY

Do remember that one's education is different from one's way. He may tell you how wrong it is to quarrel, but after a while he may be quarreling himself. It is not easy for him to change his habit. Young brothers should know that in marrying a sister, they marry her whole family. Young sisters should likewise know that in marrying a brother, they marry his whole family. You marry one person, yet in actuality you get the whole family.

Age

1. PHYSICAL

Generally speaking, women mature faster than men, but women also age faster. Women usually mature about five years ahead of men but age around ten years earlier. So in marriage, so far as the physical body is concerned, it is permissible for the man to be five, six, or even seven or eight years older than the woman.

2. MENTAL

On the other hand, there is the mental age. It is quite possible for a person to be physically matured yet mentally a child, old in body but young in mind. One may be over thirty in physical age but have a mental age of only twenty. For this reason, it is permissible for a brother whose mind matures earlier to marry a somewhat older sister whose mind is still young.

The decision rests on whether you pay more attention to physical age or to mental age. As far as physical age goes, it is better for the brother to be older than the sister. But as far as mental age is concerned, it is all right for a sister to be older than the brother. This is something each one has to decide for himself or herself.

Temperament, Interest, and Goal

The above five considerations are those matters that have more to do with the physical side. Beginning with the item now before us, we shall consider those things that are more concerned with nature or character.

For a marriage to be successful, there must not only be physical attraction but also proximity of temperament, interests, and goals. If natures and interests are too far apart, the family will eventually lose its peace and both the husband and the wife will suffer. Young people should know that natural or physical attraction is only temporary, but natures are more permanent.

Love among unbelievers is mostly natural attraction. It is not the love which the Bible mentions. There is natural attraction in love, but natural or physical attraction by itself is not love. Love includes natural attraction, but it also includes proximity of temperament. Hence, love possesses two fundamental elements: natural attraction and proximity of temperament and interests.

You may seem to love someone because there is a natural attraction to the person. Yet you do not really like the person, for you feel that whatever he or she does is different from what you would do. Your opposite party may not like what you like, and you may not like what that one likes. This shows a disparity of natures.

1. LOVE

For example, one of the two loves people very much. He or she treats others with kindness and affection, esteeming everybody as lovely. But the opposite party is quite cold and indifferent toward people, lacking in love and sympathy. Immediately you see trouble on both sides, for there is a conflict of natures. If you who love people and treat people kindly and affectionately are married to a husband or wife who also loves people and treats people kindly and affectionately, then you two will find great interest in taking care of people. You will both feel how easy marriage is. It is like you are sailing west and the current is also flowing westward; you just ride on the current. But if you are married to a person who is cold and void of feeling, you will be pulling in one direction while he or she pulls in the other direction. You feel you must bear with your spouse, and your spouse certainly tries to endure you. You endure the other's stinginess as the other one endures your liberality. This is not very harmonious.

2. KINDNESS

Some people are not only loving but also kind. Kindness means reluctance to hurt or offend others and always to think or feel for other people. Life becomes meaningful when you choose a husband or a wife who shows the same temperament as you. You both are kind and thoughtful toward others, taking delight in saving people's feelings, having no pleasure in embarrassing others. It is again as if you were sailing in one direction and the water pushes you forward. But what if you marry a person of an opposite nature? Then you will find much difficulty in marriage. For instance, if you are one who is kind not only to people but even to cats and dogs while your spouse loves neither people nor animals, this will create a great problem in the family. Both of you will be pulling in opposite directions.

3. GENEROSITY

A person who is most generous will put on the table everything he or she has if a brother or a sister comes to the house. But if that one should marry another who counts every meal eaten by friends, that person will not have an easy home life. This difficulty is not due to a moral deficiency but to a temperamental one. Some people by nature feel hurt when their food is consumed by other people. They may purposely withhold the good and put something else on the table for guests. This is a problem of temperament, not of morals.

4. CANDID OR CAUTIOUS

Some brothers by nature are frank; they like candor. Some sisters are cautious by nature; they love to see others being discreet. Here again is a conflict of temperament. It is not that one way is right and the other way wrong. There is no moral question at all, just a difficulty of temperament. One is so cautious that she tends to hide everything, while the other is so candid that he inclines to disclose all. Both are beautiful. Let not the cautious criticize the candid, nor the candid the cautious. The candid feels his feet are being dragged by the cautious, but at the same time the cautious is keenly aware of someone having traveled too fast. Both suffer.

5. REFLECTIVE OR IMPULSIVE

Some people are quite reflective. They ponder everything carefully and deeply. But other people do things without asking for an explanation. They stop to think *after* they have done something. Again, this is not a moral problem but only a difference of disposition. Let them not judge each other. Rather let the reflective seek for a reflective life-partner and the thoughtless a thoughtless mate. This will make life together much smoother.

6. EXACTING IN WORDS

Some are so very exacting in speech that they terrify people. Every word must be uttered exactly right. Others may not be so careful. They are not altogether careless nor do they have the intention to be inaccurate, but their speech is just not too exact. Once again, these differences do not constitute a moral problem, rather they are a temperamental one. The careful one may unnecessarily accuse the other of lying, while the latter may advise the former one that it would be better not to speak at all. Frankly, if every word in the world had to be so accurately spoken, there might not be more than twenty sentences uttered. So the disparity of disposition is indeed a big problem.

7. ACTIVE OR INACTIVE

Some people have a vivacious temperament while others have a calm temperament. There is nothing wrong with either of these.

There is no moral problem; it is simply a difference of temperament. But for an especially lively sister to be married to an exceedingly cool brother will no doubt cause trouble in the family. Sooner or later, they will try to make this temperamental problem into a moral problem. They will magnify each other's peculiarity. I personally know a husband who likes to sit at home, but he has married a sister who delights in visiting others. As a matter of fact, I know quite a few cases like that in Shanghai. The husband finds it quite unbearable to follow his wife and go around to people's houses. The alternative is to stay home and watch the house for her. He can endure this situation a few times, but he cannot endure it forever. When he comes home, he rarely finds her. This is not a moral issue but a temperamental problem which was overlooked at the time of marriage.

8. NEAT OR SLOPPY

A certain sister I know is especially neat. She follows after her husband and straightens up everything after him. But the husband takes pleasure in sloppiness. One day I visited their home and found the husband throwing the pillow on the floor and turning over the chair. I asked him why he was doing these things. His answer was that he was extremely happy because today his wife had gone to her parents' home. He had been so frustrated by her cleanliness that now he got release by making everything sloppy!

9. SIMILAR NATURES

Christians should know that love has two fundamental elements: natural attraction and proximity of natures. So in choosing a mate, Christians need to choose not only those to whom they are naturally attracted but also those who have a somewhat similar temperament. Do not neglect the latter while being engrossed with the former.

I met a couple in Shanghai who were always quarreling. I asked the husband why he married her in the first place. He replied that when he first saw her, he was attracted by her two raven-dark eyes. This was natural attraction. But soon after marriage, those dark eyes were forgotten. All he remembered now was that she enjoyed laughing while he liked quietness, she acted quickly while he reacted slowly. Remember, a temperamental problem is a permanent problem.

When young brothers and sisters are choosing their mates, they should not look at natural attraction only. It is true that there must be natural attraction, but it is also true that this alone is not enough. They must take note of proximity of natures. Natural attraction will soon disappear. Though it may tempt you to marriage, it will not sustain your marriage. It may stir you to initiate a move, but it does not have the power to sustain that move.

10. HEAVEN OR HELL

There is a saying: a person may have two heavens or two hells. A happy family is like heaven, while an unhappy family is like hell. An unbeliever may have two hells; he may live in hell while alive and descend to hell after death. A Christian too may live in hell today if there is no harmony in his family; in the future, though, he will ascend to heaven.

I remember especially one brother whose wife quarreled with everybody. She appeared to be quite spiritual and could pray well. But when her temper was stirred, no one could outtalk her. She often quarreled with her neighbors, and her husband was always having to apologize to them for her actions. Whenever he returned home, he would inquire if she had quarreled with some neighbor or other so he could make amends. As a matter of fact, she did quarrel every day. If only that brother had married a quiet woman and that sister had married a passionate man, their families would not have been subject to so much disturbance.

11. Acceptance of the Other

Many have the wrong concept of thinking they can change someone else's temperament. This never happens. For the Holy Spirit to change a person's character takes lots of time; how could you, then, succeed in this impossible task? Even marriage has not the power to change one's nature. Many brothers and sisters, aware of the disparity of their temperaments, hopefully wait for a change. But the expected change does not come. If there is one hope in the world which is doomed to despair, this one certainly is. I have yet to see a husband who has changed his wife, or a wife who has changed her husband. As I once said, in marriage you can only get ready-made goods, not made-to-order goods. Whatever the brother or the sister is, that is what you get. Before marriage you should first observe whether the brother or sister's present condition is commendable or not, for you cannot afterward expect to change the temperament of your marriage partner to suit yours.

12. Warning

Pardon me for saying a little more. In over a decade of working in Shanghai, one-fourth of my time has been spent in solving family problems. Out of this experience, I emphatically sound the warning that people with different natures should not be joined together. To do so will not be good for the husband, the wife, or their children. The children of such a marriage will be torn in their loyalty; they will not know with whom they should stand. It may even affect their salvation.

Weaknesses

The above matters refer only to differences of nature without any involvement of a moral problem; now, though, we shall see that human beings do have weaknesses.

1. WEAKNESS A MORAL PROBLEM

What is a weakness? Some people are lazy, while some are diligent. We know diligence is a virtue but laziness is a weakness. Some are very accurate in their use of words. This indeed is a virtue. But some are not only a little too careless in speech but also actually love to add words to what they say. They are telling lies. This is a weakness in character. Again, some are tight-lipped. They do not like to talk too much—and this is good. But some like to criticize and to teach; this cannot be considered a virtue; rather, it is a weakness. The spreading of rumors is more than a temperamental problem for it involves morals. Wherever morals are involved, there is a weakness which needs to be dealt with before God. For example, some people do things quickly and others act slowly. This is a temperamental problem. But if anyone should be so quick as to be careless or so slow as to be undependable, he has a weakness.

2. KNOWLEDGE OF THE OTHER'S WEAKNESSES

What should one do about the weaknesses of the opposite party? This is rather hard for an outsider to decide. Before young brothers and sisters marry, they need to find out the weaknesses of their proposed partner. These must be found before they are engaged, not afterward. It is wrong to look for the weaknesses of the opposite party after marriage. It is more than wrong: it is foolish. After marriage is too late to do such a thing. Once married, the husband and the wife should be as blind and deaf as possible. Even without looking, you will see plenty; what, then, if you should search carefully? Marriage should not be used as an opportunity for finding fault. You should not use your eyes after you are married. But before you are engaged, at the time you are choosing your mate, do not be so blinded by natural attraction that you fail to notice the weaknesses of the other person. Do not be so eager for marriage that you cannot see any weakness in the other party.

3. BEARABLE OR UNBEARABLE

There are two alternatives about weaknesses: either they are bearable or they are not. If there is an unbearable weakness, then marriage should not be considered. But if the weaknesses are bearable, then you may consider marriage. However, all weaknesses must be discovered before engagement. What is the use of finding fault after marriage? To do so will only cause your family life to deteriorate, since it is not possible for you to change it.

4. MUST NOT BE SHARED

Let me put in a warning: do not think that people with similar weaknesses can live together. Many people fancy that they can live with someone who has the same weakness but not with someone of a different weakness. There is no such thing. It is even more difficult for people of a similar weakness to live together. If it is purely a temperamental disparity, the conscience is not involved. But if it is a weakness, the conscience will be involved. Then both the brother and the sister will suffer doubly;

they will suffer for themselves as well as for the other party. Thus, both their difficulty and their responsibility will be doubled. Temperament must be shared but weakness cannot be.

Let this be pointed out: though a weakness may be pardonable, it may also be unbearable. Further, it is better that the weaknesses of two persons not be the same.

Character

For a marriage to be successful, it is necessary for the two to have mutual respect. If either one of them looks down on the other, the family is doomed. The husband must respect his wife's character; the wife must appreciate the quality of her husband's character. This is not a matter of temperament or of weakness, but of character.

For example: it is pardonable for a wife to tell a lie occasionally; but if she is dishonest and often lies, it is a reflection on her character. Or, for another example, how can a husband command the respect of his wife if he is so selfish that he only thinks of himself? The husband in a family should at least have some admirable qualities. Character is different from temperament. If there is nothing to respect, the family is finished. A disparity in temperament makes the going hard enough, but a lack of admirable character destroys the very foundation of a home. Who can save a family in which the husband distrusts the wife and vice versa?

Some people are quite cruel; they treat people harshly. They do not care how others feel, but are concerned only with their own feelings. This is not a matter of disparity in temperament but is a defect in character. A character that does not command respect brings failure to a marriage.

41

Some people have no control over themselves. They are loose in their lives. They freely lose their temper. Why are they ill-tempered? Because they are selfish, seeking their own self-satisfaction. To some people, a display of temper is very satisfying. But to the second party, such a questionable character may occasion the rise of contempt.

A mean husband, a wife who takes advantage of everything—these are distinct character defects rather than weaknesses. If one is choosing a mate, he must observe whether he can stand the character of the other party. Hence, before marriage find out if there is mutual respect. Especially in the marriage of God's children, admirable character is essential. One who lacks in admirable character is not qualified to be married. There must be that which is commendable in the sight of God.

Congeniality

Another point to be noticed in the realm of personality is whether the proposed wife or husband is able to live with other people. Marriage is a living together. Some people are quite peculiar, and cannot dwell peaceably with others. If a man has been unable to live with his parents or brothers and sisters, then how could you expect a happy married life with him? Or if a woman has always been striving with people, you could hardly hope for a successful family life by marrying her.

A fundamental condition for marriage is the congeniality of the person. If one cannot live with other people, that one also cannot live with you. Would such a person despise everyone else and esteem only you? No, you too will be despised after marriage.

For example: if a sister reaching the age of marriage

tells people how she has been ill-treated by her father, mother, brothers and sisters, yes, by everyone, you will know of a certainty that later on she will tell the same thing about you. This sister lacks the power to live with others.

If one is highly congenial, he or she will be easy to live with. This is truly quite an important condition.

Consecration

The first set of items in this lesson on mating touched on the physical side; the second set dealt with matters of personality or character—the soulical side; now in the third set we shall consider the spiritual side.

1. SAME PURPOSE

A Christian must not marry an unbeliever. We must see that to attain to the highest meaning of marriage, there must be oneness of spiritual purpose in addition to physical attraction and complementary natures. This means that both must have the desire to serve God. Both must be fully committed to the Lord. Both must live for God. This is more important than having an admirable character. Though the latter cannot be omitted, the former is absolutely indispensable. In big things and small things, both must live for the Lord.

Such a marriage has a solid foundation, for the two parties have a strong bond of unity before God.

2. CHRIST AS LORD

In a family having oneness of purpose, there is no striving as to who stands in the position of head and who obeys. Christ is the head who is to be obeyed. Christ is the

Lord of the house. The question of saving face is altogether eliminated. Many husbands and wives quarrel, not because they care for right and wrong, but because they want to save their faces. Were they both consecrated Christians, this problem would be non-existent. Both would be willing to lose face before the Lord. Both would be able to confess their fault. Since both desire most of all to do the will of God, everything can be settled on that basis.

Young brothers and sisters should know that they must be fully consecrated. If both parties to a proposed marriage serve the Lord with all their hearts, the probability of success in their marriage is exceedingly high. Even though there may be some natural differences and even though physical attraction may somewhat fade, the family will prosper without hindrance.

May young brothers and sisters see that there are conditions for marriage. Simply speaking, these conditions may be divided along three lines: the physical or external, the psychological, and the spiritual. These three need to be placed in their proper respective positions.

Conclusion

It needs to be emphatically stated that the second generation family has much to do with the second generation church. If we take good care of the families of the next generation, then we have also taken good care of the church of that generation. If the families of the generation coming up are full of problems, we workers will have to spend our time settling family affairs. We cannot alter the situation for those who are already married. All we can do is to persuade them to be more adjustable, more patient, more affectionate, and more loving. But for those who are not yet married, our expectation is that they should have a good family life.

When I was in England, I met a number of families in which both the husbands and the wives served the Lord and walked in the way of God together. Such a situation is truly beautiful to watch. To see a couple following God with one accord is a wonderful sight. Let the older brothers and sisters help the younger ones in this matter so that the latter may avoid many mistakes. May God bless all the brothers and sisters.

HUSBAND AND WIFE

Wives, be in subjection to your husbands, as is fitting in the Lord. Husbands, love your wives, and be not bitter against them.

Col. 3:18-19

In like manner, ye wives, be in subjection to your own husbands; that, even if any obey not the word, they may without the word be gained by the behavior of their wives; beholding your chaste behavior coupled with fear. Whose adorning let it not be the outward adorning of braiding the hair, and of wearing jewels of gold, or of putting on apparel; but let it be the hidden man of the heart, in the incorruptible apparel of a meek and quiet spirit, which is in the sight of God of great price. For after this manner aforetime the holy women also, who hoped in God, adorned themselves, being in subjection to their own husbands: as Sarah obeyed Abraham, calling him lord: whose children ye now are, if ye do well, and are not put in fear by any terror. Ye husbands, in like manner, dwell with your wives according to knowledge, giving honor unto the woman, as unto the weaker vessel, as being also joint-heirs of the grace of life; to the end that your prayers be not hindered.

1 Pet. 3:1-7

Wives, be in subjection unto your own husbands, as unto the Lord. For the husband is head of the wife, as Christ also is the head of the church, being himself the saviour of the body.

Eph. 5:22–23

In the last lesson we mentioned how to choose a mate. Such a lesson primarily seems to be addressed to young brothers and sisters. But not all in our midst are young; some are already married. Further, there will be more married people saved in the future. The Bible does have definite teaching for these married people. There are passages which give instruction on how to be husbands and other passages tell how to be wives. Before a person is married, he or she should choose the most suitable person to marry. But after one is married, the man must learn before God how to be a husband even as the woman must learn how to be a wife. By so learning, problems in the home and in the church will be lessened

Spend Time to Learn

First of all, the married person—husband or wife—must see that to be a husband or a wife is a most serious matter.

1. A SERIOUS MATTER

Before a person can enter into a profession, he must be properly prepared. To be a physician requires college plus several more years of training; a teacher needs to spend four or five years in a teachers college; an engineer must at least finish a four-year course in college; a nurse must study four years in a nursing school. Is it not strange, then, that one can be a husband or a wife without even one day of training? No wonder there are so many poor husbands and poor wives. They have never learned how! If I am sick, would I trust myself to the care of a medically untrained doctor or nurse? If I need someone to teach a child, would I ask the help of an unschooled person? If I am going to build a house, would I dare engage an unqualified architect? How, then, can I think it well for a man to be a husband or a woman to be a wife who has never learned how?

All too often our parents do not teach us how to be husbands or wives. When we reach the right age or have a job or find the other half, we just go ahead and get married. We simply marry when we have the money or ability to support a family. But this lack of preparation is where the future problems of the family begin. Suddenly two persons are drawn into matrimony as if they were meant to be husband and wife. Actually, though, they have not the slightest preparation for such a joint enterprise. How can such a family be successful? Therefore, it is our responsibility to impress upon new believers the necessity for preparation in anything we undertake during our lifetime.

Another impression new believers need to be given is that the task of being a husband or a wife is the most difficult in the world. Any other kind of work is confined to certain hours, but this is a twenty-four hour job. All other work has a retirement age; only this task does not. This is *the* most demanding and serious job of all.

2. A Remedial Lesson

Since so many have already married without having had any training, we must let bygones be bygones. We need to concentrate now on how to improve the existing situation. Seeing how serious it is to have a family, husbands should be willing to take remedial steps to learn how to be husbands; wives should do the same on their part.

Even if a person is trained and treats the family as a professional would, he or she still may be subject to failure. How much more is a family doomed, then, if a person's attitude toward it is very unprofessional, not at all serious. A person should put his or her entire energy into the marriage and be more diligently occupied with it than with other things. The family cannot escape failure if it is treated lightly. In order to make your family a success before God, you must take it seriously and spend time on it. Whatever failure there has been must be turned into success. Marriage is so serious that it has to be successful.

Therefore, all married brothers and sisters should learn to take up their responsibility before God. Since marriage is more difficult than any other profession, no one should delay to diligently learn how.

Close Your Eyes

The first thing to learn after marriage is to close your eyes that you may not see.

When two people live together as husband and wife, day after day, year after year, without vacation or sick leave, each one has plenty of time to find out the weaknesses of the opposite party. So, as soon as you are married, you must close your eyes. The aim of marriage is not to discover the weaknesses of your life partner. Remember, she is your wife, not your student; he is your husband, not your apprentice. You are *not* required to find the difficulties and weaknesses of your mate in order to help and correct them. A family should be built on a solid foundation. Hence, before you are married, you have to open your eyes wide so as to understand everything, even the possible difficulties. But after you are married, you must not seek to understand any more. If you want to split hairs, you have plenty of opportunity to do so. Since God has put you together, you both have plenty of time, perhaps fifty years, to discover the weaknesses of the other one. For this reason, the first thing the married brothers and sisters should do is close their eyes to the difficulties and weaknesses of their counterparts. You will see enough without looking! How many more difficulties there will be if you seek them on purpose.

In joining two people together as husband and wife, God has arranged that there be subjection and love in the family. He has not asked the husband and wife to find and correct each other's faults. He has not set up husbands to be instructors to their wives or wives to be teachers to their husbands. A husband need not change his wife or a wife her husband. Whatever the manner of person you marry, you must expect to live with that for life. Do not purposely look for difficulties and weaknesses with a view to helping. Such a concept of helping is basically wrong. Married people should learn to close their eyes. They should learn to love and not to help or correct.

Learn to Accommodate

To accommodate is a lesson which needs to be learned immediately after marriage. No matter how much alike the dispositions of the couple are, sooner or later they will discover lots of differences. They still will have different viewpoints, likes and dislikes, opinions and inclinations.

Hence they must learn soon after they are married to accommodate themselves to each other.

1. Go Halfway

What is meant by accommodation? It means that I will meet the other party halfway. It is best if this is mutual. But in case it is not reciprocal, you yourself can at least go half of the way. However, many problems will be solved if you can leave your position and go over all the way. When this is not possible, it is still good to meet your partner halfway. In other words, after the brother and the sister have become husband and wife, they both should learn to make adjustments in all things. If you can adjust all the way, fine; if not, adapt yourself at least half of the way. Learn to go out and meet the other. Do not insist on your opinions, but be willing to change your views. Although you have your ideas, learn to accommodate yourself to the thoughts of your life partner.

If a young couple learn to accommodate themselves to each other during the first five years of marriage, they will have a peaceful and happy home five years later. If during the first five years, neither of them learns what accommodation is, that is, neither meets the other halfway, that family can hardly be expected to be harmonious. Marriage is not a simple matter. To have a good marriage requires both time and effort.

To accommodate means to discover what bothers the other. Some are especially afraid of noise, while others become nervous when it is silent. Some cannot live without lots of activity, but others can hardly live with it. Here is where accommodation must come in. One should lower the sound, while the other should allow some noise. Thus they meet halfway. Suppose the wife is extremely tidy while the husband is very lazy. To require the lazy one to wholly follow the tidy one may cause him some day to throw everything around and shout that his wife should go to her parents' home! Or the wife, having found that her husband is so untidy, may welcome the opportunity to return to her parents' home!

2. LEARN TO DENY YOURSELF

As Christians, we must learn to deny ourselves. To deny oneself means to accommodate oneself to others. Both the husband and the wife should learn to be more accommodating. Then there will at least be peace in the family. Where there is self-denial, there will be accommodation. Where self-denial is absent, accommodation will also be absent.

Young believers ought to see that being accommodating in the family is not just in a few dozen things; it may cover hundreds or thousands of things. This is what G. H. Pember calls the discipline of the family. Since there is much occasion in the family for accommodation, you may say there is discipline in family life. You have to learn to lay aside your own opinion and to accept the other's view.

Be Appreciative and Sensitive

Once you are married you should learn at once to appreciate the strengths of your partner.

1. NOTICE THE OTHER'S STRENGTHS

We must not only be accommodating and close our eyes to weaknesses, we must also learn to appreciate the strengths of the opposite party. We should be sensitive to things that are well done. Family relationships will greatly suffer if the husband does not know how to appreciate his wife, or if the wife does not value her husband. Remember, we need neither flatter our wives nor seek to satisfy our husbands' vanity. What is needed is to appreciate each other. Learn to see the strengths, the virtues, the beauty of the other.

There is a responsible brother in one local assembly who is well spoken of by everybody. But you cannot ask his wife about him for she always complains that he is the worst one. She often criticizes her husband, saying he is not fit to be a responsible brother. Why is this? Perhaps it is because she likes to direct her husband. Being rejected in this, she accuses him of being unfit to be a responsible brother. All the brothers and sisters in the meeting are submissive to him; only the one who is his wife is not. How can such a family as this be beautiful?

The situation may be the other way. With the exception of the husband, most people may feel that the woman is a good wife. I remember one year when I was in Peking, several people were talking together and highly praising a certain sister. In the middle of their conversation, her husband came in. They quite naturally continued praising that sister, but her husband said not a word. His silence conveyed the thought of, "Who knows that I have married the wrong person?" Such a thought certainly destroys the family.

2. Make Your Appreciation Known

A husband's appreciation of his wife must not be less than anyone else's. His appreciation may not be higher, but at least it should not be less than other people's. Why did you marry her if you appreciate her value so little? Either your perception was wrong then or it is wrong now.

The same applies to the wife. Why did you marry that man if you feel he is the wrong person? You yourself must be wrong. To have a happy family, mutual appreciation is essential. Let it not be that others praise your life partner while you criticize. Notice your partner's strengths and be aware of his or her virtues. Whenever opportunity offers itself, confess publicly what you have observed and felt. This is not being pretentious, for you are telling the truth. When the husband and the wife appreciate each other in this way, the family tie is strengthened.

If there is not such expression of appreciation, lots of misunderstandings and problems will be produced. In England there was a brother married to a sister who never told her that she had done something well. Naturally this sister was always worrying as to whether she had failed as a wife and as a Christian. She worried herself to tuberculosis and to death. While she was dying her husband said to her, "I do not know what to do if you die, for you have done so much good. What will become of this family if you die?" "Why did you not say this earlier?" asked the wife. "I always feel I am no good. I blame myself all the time. You have never once said, 'Well done.' I have worried myself to sickness and now to death." Remember, a family really needs nice words; it would be well if such nice words were frequently spoken. Husbands and wives should learn to appreciate each other and to speak nicely of each other.

I know that quite a few brothers do not do well simply because their wives are not appreciative. Their wives always say the husbands are no good; consequently the husbands become self-accusing. Their wives act as their consciences. Since those who ought to know them best— their wives—judge them as good-for-nothings, the husbands conclude that they must be no good. For this reason let it be remembered that the success or failure of a family depends much on appreciation and acknowledgement of each other's strengths and virtues as well as on restraint from noticing each other's weaknesses and difficulties.

Be Courteous

A family must be courteous to each other. It is abominable not to be courteous.

We all should be courteous to everyone. However familiar you are with a person, you will lose him as a friend if you are lacking in politeness. Paul tells us that love "doth not behave itself unseemly" (1 Cor. 13:5). Oftentimes family troubles are caused by small things. The time a person is least gracious is when he is at home. You think since your wife or your husband is the person most intimate to you, you may be less thoughtful. But you should remember that courtesy beautifies human contact. Once it is removed, all the ugly parts of life will be revealed. However familiar people are, courtesy must be maintained. One brother explained this well by saying that courtesy is like the lubricating oil put in machinery. Without courtesy there will be friction and unpleasant feelings.

1. IN WORDS

Learn to say "Thank you" or "Excuse me." Polite words such as "May I?" or "Please" should frequently be used. If you were to eliminate these words, you might not be able to make friends. How much more they are necessary in the family! Christians should remember well that "love doth not behave itself unseemly." We must learn to say these gracious words at home.

2. In Dress

Not only must your words be polite and your manner courteous, but also your dress must be tidy. Since you like to dress tidily before friends, you should also be clothed neatly in your home. You ought not behave unseemly in the matter of clothing. Avoid being careless because of familiarity. Familiarity can breed contempt. Who is as familiar as a husband and wife? Courtesy, therefore, must not be neglected. You must be dressed neatly. Do not put on disrespectful clothes while at home.

3. In Manner

In manner, there must be graciousness. It is best if you pass the plate with two hands unless it is designed for using one hand.* When you pass a knife or a pair of scissors to someone, do not point the sharp end at him. When you deliver something, do not throw it. Especially in the home should such graciousness be kept. You may save three seconds by throwing instead of handing over a thing, but the aftereffects are quite serious. Learn to be courteous.

I have had sufficient contact with families to know that if a person is polite, he or she will have few problems at home. It is almost a rule of thumb that if the husband and the wife are courteous to each other, that family at least has quietness. There will be less clinking of plates and forks. Any family void of courtesy will be full of friction.

I believe no one would visit a woman's home if she treated her friends in the same manner she assumes as a wife, nor would anyone be the man's associate if he should treat his colleagues in the same manner he exhibits as a husband. Let us tell the brothers that their wives have

---

* According to Chinese custom, this is the polite way.—*Translator*

endured what their colleagues could not bear. Tell the
sisters that their husbands have been very patient with
them, that even their friends would not be able to stand
the treatment they have given their husbands. To be
discourteous is rude and a Christian must not be rude. He
who has "learned Christ" (Eph. 4:20 Darby) cannot be a
discourteous person.

4. IN VOICE

Our voice also must be cordial. It is possible for us to say
the same words in different ways and tones. The boss uses
a certain tone in speaking to his subordinates. Friends talk
to each other in a friendly tone. Love speaks with a lovely
voice, while hate utters its words in a tone that expresses
hate. A difficulty with many people is that they use an
unpleasant voice at home because they have exhausted
their pleasant voice outside the home. They are courteous
to their colleagues at work, patient to the sick at the
hospital, and careful when speaking to their pupils at
school; but they do not care what voice they use at home.
If they used the same voice in the office as at home, they
would be fired within two days. How can a home be
maintained if they use only a rude tone of voice there?

If the tone is not right, the family will not be peaceful.
Remember, no careless word, no hard or harsh voice, no
proud or self-piteous tone, no martyr-like or self-loving
intonation should be used at home. "Love doth not behave
itself unseemly," not even in voice.

Let Love Grow

For a family to be successful, love must grow continuously and not be allowed to die.

1. Nourish Your Love

The young often ask if love can die. I think I may answer here that love may die and die easily. Like a living thing, love needs to be nourished. It will die if there is no supply. Starve it and it will die; nourish it and it will grow.

Love is the foundation of the family as well as of marriage. Love leads two people into marriage; love also keeps them together in the family. It can easily grow if properly nourished, but it can also easily die if starved. Many have love before their marriage, but then after marriage they begin to starve it. No wonder their love gradually dies out. Love needs to be fed by accommodation, sacrifice, self-denial, understanding, sympathy, and forgiveness. All of these must be repeated over and over. If it is nourished, love can grow beautifully. But if people do not seek the pleasure of others but think only of their own welfare, their love will soon be starved and die.

It is painful to marry without love; it is tragic to have a family without love. One may be able to endure a family without love when he is young or even middle aged, but in his old age he will be chilled by the coldness of the family. The difference is great. Learn, therefore, to feed the family with love when you are yet young or middle-aged. Try to nourish your love. Then the home will be full of love.

2. Avoid Things Unpleasant to the Other

Every married person should try to find out what the other party is most afraid of and most dislikes. Never live a loose and careless life. Everybody has that which he abhors or fears. If your partner has a moral weakness, I hope there will be mutual accommodation so as to correct the situation. If it is not a moral weakness, I would suggest that instead of meeting the other halfway, you go all the way.

Several years ago I read a story about a husband in the United States who accused his wife in court of cruelty. The story sounded humorous, yet it was most awful. The man in the story couldn't stand a monotonous sound. At first he and his wife loved each other deeply. But after they had been married less than two years, the family relationship began to deteriorate. His wife liked to knit. It was the monotonous sound of knitting that wracked his nerves. He suffered this sound for seven years. Finally he went to court to accuse his wife of mental cruelty toward him. The judge explained that since knitting was not a crime, this was not a sufficient cause for divorce. However, the man stated that he had loved his wife before they were married and had looked on her as a lamb. But one year after marriage she had started knitting and had kept on ever since. So today he could not bear the sight of knitting and, furthermore, he felt inclined to kill every lamb he saw on the street. He told the judge if a divorce were not granted, he could not be held responsible for killing lambs in the street. This case was an actual one. The wife had thought there was nothing wrong with knitting, but the man so abhorred it that it made him ready to kill a lamb.

Remember, everyone has that which he hates or fears. Usually this does not involve a moral problem. It is just the person's characteristic. For a family to be successful, neither the husband nor the wife should do that seemingly unimportant thing which is important to the other person.

I have had much contact with families in Shanghai and in other places and I have found that points of conflict in the family are usually over insignificant matters. To outsiders and to friends, those matters are really tiny things. Yet they exhaust all the patience a person has when they happen constantly in the family.

Let new believers see that it is a very delicate thing for two people to dwell together. It is not easy and therefore should not be taken lightly. If what you consider insignificant happens to be something your life partner abhors, for you to do that is to subject the latter to mental cruelty.

Be Unselfish

Another important condition of family life is to not be selfish.

1. SEEK TO PLEASE THE OTHER

If you are married, live like a married person. You should not live like an unmarried person. The Word of God says: "he that is married is careful for the things of the world, how he may please his wife. . . . she that is married is careful for the things of the world, how she may please her husband" (1 Cor. 7:33-34). The greatest difficulty a family faces is probably selfishness.

I recall that there was a pastor in the United States who performed seven hundred and fifty marriages in his life. During each wedding ceremony, he would exhort the newlyweds not to be selfish. There must be love, not selfishness, in married life. During his old age, he wrote letters to those he had married, inquiring about their current situation. There still were over seven hundred of these couples living. The replies he received were unanimous: their family life was happy because they were not selfish. Such a situation was quite unusual in the States, for at that time one out of four marriages was ending in divorce.

We must learn how to feel for the other—empathize with the pain or joy, the fear or hate, the difficulty or inclination of the opposite party. One who is subjective cannot be a good husband or a good wife. Subjective people are all selfish.

2. SACRIFICE YOUR LIKES

One basic condition which marriage implies is sacrifice. One must learn to please the other. To do this, you cannot be subjective. It is not whether *you* like it or not, but whether your partner likes it or not. Learn to find out the likes and dislikes, thoughts or viewpoints of your counterpart. Learn to stand on the other side that you may understand both your opposite party and yourself. As much as possible sacrifice your own feeling, opinion, and viewpoint. Seek to understand, to deny yourself, and to love. In this way family problems will be greatly diminished.

Many marriages have the following difficulty: the husband of the house thinks of nothing but that he is the center of the universe around whom everything else revolves. He marries a wife in order to better his life and his welfare. Such a family is bound to have trouble. Likewise, the wife of a house may think of herself as the center of the universe for whom everybody else lives. She marries a man whom she thinks may realize her objective of being served. Such a marriage is doomed to failure, for it is a marriage motivated by self-profit.

Permit Freedom, Privacy, and Private Possessions

In the family, one must allow the other party certain freedom, privacy, and private possessions.

1. Don't Be a Jailor

In some families, the wives have no privileges whatever. On the other hand, in some of today's modern families the husbands have no privileges. Such families undoubtedly have troubles. To be a good husband or a good wife, you must remember that you can love any person in the world except a jailor. No one can love a jailor, for no one wants to be a prisoner. You cannot love the sentinel who watches the door. How can you love the one who causes you to lose your freedom? Many a husband behaves toward his wife like a prison warden. For such a husband to look for love from his wife is like a warden expecting the prisoner to love him. You expect too much; there is no possibility of it. The same is true with wives who act as wardens to their husbands. Wardens inspire fear, not love. No person can afford to have all his freedom taken away from him. Although marriage does cause a man and a woman to lose freedom, it must be remembered that not all freedom is lost. The husband does not give all his freedom to the wife, nor does the wife yield all her freedom to the husband. If the husband expects his wife to give all her freedom to him, then he must know that either his wife will fear him or hate him.

2. God Gives Us Freedom

No one wants to lose his or her total freedom. The desire for freedom is a part of human nature. God Himself gives us freedom. This can be seen in the fact that there is no hedge around the gate of hell. It can also be seen in that there are no cherubim's flaming swords around the tree of the knowledge of good and evil. If God did not want to give man freedom, he would have surrounded the tree of the knowledge of good and evil with the flaming swords of the cherubim so that man could not eat its fruit. But God did not and does not violate man's freedom. Likewise, every husband should give his wife some freedom of choice, and every wife should give her husband the same freedom. Once you take away freedom and decide for the other person, you will receive back either fear or, even worse, hate. When freedom is lost, either hate comes or, at the least, fear rises up.

In the family, both the husband and the wife should learn to give freedom to the other. Each of them should have his or her own time, money, and things. Just because there is a husband-and-wife relationship, these things should not be usurped. You need to learn to keep your place. Otherwise, a small thing like this can cause a big problem.

3. RESPECT THE RIGHT TO PRIVACY

Every husband and every wife should be allowed to have his or her own privacy. This is perfectly legitimate. It is permissible for the left hand to do something without notifying the right hand (see Matt. 6:3). Learn, therefore, to respect each individual's privilege of some privacy. This will help the family avoid many troubles.

Learn to Solve Problems

The matter now before us is how to solve family problems. Husbands and wives cannot avoid having some differences and difficulties. Since both are grown-ups and both are children of God, they need to understand first where their differences and difficulties are. Before any difficulty can be solved, one needs to know where the problem is. After identifying where the problem is, they need to find the solution to it.

1. FIND A FAIR SOLUTION

The way a problem is solved must be fair. If a solution is not fair, it will not last. No one is able to endure to the end. Do not expect your opposite party to endure forever. Out of ten Christians, you might find one who can suffer long; the other nine just cannot bear up indefinitely. If the solution to a problem is unfair, the problem will explode again when opportunity comes. When I was in Shanghai, I helped solve some difficulties among the brethren. They often wondered why such a tiny thing should create such a big furor. Their surprise was caused by their lack of experience. A small thing becoming a big thing is due to what has happened before, not to the thing itself. The explosion finally comes when the accumulation of irritation gets to be too much. The spark may be ignited over a small thing, but the cause has been amassing for years. Thus, do not treat something as small, but find out in what way the earlier solution was unfair. The explosion comes only when patience has been exhausted.

2. COUNSEL TOGETHER

It is best for the husband and the wife to talk things over with each other. Outsiders should not interfere at the beginning, though there may be occasion to help later on. First let the two people exchange their views freely. The news should not be known to others and travel far and wide while it has not yet been discussed at home. Sometimes things concerning the husband are known twenty miles away and yet the husband is ignorant of them. Things between a husband and wife ought to be told to each other. Provide opportunity for such a family council. Let your partner finish speaking before you speak. Guard against the talkative one monopolizing the conversation. The husband should listen to the wife and the wife to the husband.

If the husband would only once listen to his wife and the wife to her husband, many things could be solved. All too frequently, though, the wife says all she wants to say but then never listens to her husband, and vice versa. Try to listen once; oftentimes by so doing the problem can be easily settled.

When you are sitting down to talk, discuss your conflicts objectively. If they are brought out subjectively, the conference will not be successful. The purpose of your talking is to find out what is right. Neither one of you knows who is right, so both of you must be intent on finding the truth. You should both talk and afterward both pray. Through prayer seek a solution. Ask the Lord to make you both understand where the trouble lies. Usually by the time you pray the second time, most matters will be solved. The problem of many is that they have not sat down and listened objectively. When they do, their difficulty is half solved; they will soon be able to discover the real trouble spot.

During the first few years of marriage such a family council should be held two or three times; after that it may seldom be needed. Thus most family difficulties can be understood and solved. This is something many families have tried successfully, and consequently many problems have been solved.

Confess and Forgive

In family life, husband and wife often need to confess to each other and forgive each other. They should not just casually pass over their faults but should confess them. One should confess one's own fault and forgive the other's fault.

1. Confess Your Sin

If a Christian sins, the basic principle is neither to cover nor to only repent but also to confess to the one wronged. To cover up and determine not to do it again is not good enough. A Christian should confess his sin to the other person, saying, "I have done wrong in such-and-such a matter." All faults must be confessed. Every time a wrong is done in the family, it must be repented of and confessed.

2. Forgive the Other

When you are at fault, confess. But what should you do when the fault is your partner's? Remember, your family relationship is like all other Christian relationships. When your counterpart is wrong, learn to forgive instead of probing. For love "taketh not account of evil" (1 Cor. 13:5). Love does not record every wrong; rather, love learns to forgive. As soon as a sin is forgiven, it is forgotten. Love will not behave as Peter in Matthew 18 did, counting every sin and limiting the measure of forgiveness. True forgiveness takes no account of time; as soon as a sin is forgiven it is forgotten. For a family to be successful, there must be forgiveness.

Seek the Church's Help

When a family is having trouble, it is best to solve it within the family, perhaps in the family council. There should be confession and forgiveness. To bring in a third party tends to increase the difficulty. Hence try your best to solve it simply. Do not let it become too complicated.

Sometimes, though, you may want to bring a certain matter to the church. You should not, however, do this arbitrarily. First, the husband needs to get his wife's permission, and the wife her husband's. Since neither of you know how to solve the problem, you decide to seek the help of the church. The purpose is not to fight before the church, but rather to ask the church to help solve the problem. Both husband and wife should come before the church and both should speak. Both should come willingly, saying, "We are Christians. We want the church to help us find out where we are wrong. We will each of us tell the church how we feel." Since both parties are glad to receive help from the church, their problem will be solved easily. Such a procedure does not aim at revenge or at disclosure of the other's fault, but at a sincere desire to know where the fault really lies.

Live Together before God

To solve family problems and to live happily together, it is necessary for the couple to have a positive life together before God. Especially parents with children need to have a time to pray together. Every couple needs such a time to wait on God and to deliberate spiritual things. Whether it is the husband or the wife, both must gladly accept the judgment of God's light. The husband must not try to save his face, nor the wife her's. There must be fellowship together. Spend time in praying and deliberating together. In order to have a good family, both must live before God.

A Good Church Comes from Good Families

We have mentioned these various conditions so that young brothers and sisters may learn together in their family life. May you not be careless or foolish. Carelessness will bring trouble both to the family and to the church. Remember, unless one dwells in unity in the family with one's spouse, that person cannot be of one accord with brothers and sisters in the church. How can one quarrel with one's partner at home and sing hallelujah in the church? He who lives in a good way at home will also live well in the church. A good church will have behind it the support of good families. If both the husbands and the wives are in a good place together, the church will have little trouble.

PARENTHOOD

Children, obey your parents in the Lord: for this is right. Honor thy father and mother (which is the first commandment with promise), that it may be well with thee, and thou mayest live long on the earth. And, ye fathers, provoke not your children to wrath: but nurture them in the chastening and admonition of the Lord.

Eph. 6:1-4

Children, obey your parents in all things, for this is well-pleasing in the Lord. Fathers, provoke not your children, that they be not discouraged.

Col. 3:20-21

Great Responsibility

The Old Testament does not seem to have much teaching on parenthood other than in Proverbs, but in the New Testament Paul gives definite instruction on how to be parents. Parenthood is stressed in the New Testament. Though the New Testament does have some teaching on how to be children, it does not seem to be as strong as is the teaching on parenthood. The words for parents in both

71

Ephesians 6 and Colossians 3 are stronger than those for children. God pays more attention to the parents than to the children. Man needs to learn how to be a parent.

A summary of all the words in the Bible on parenthood would come to this: nurture the children in the chastening and admonition of the Lord and do not provoke their wrath lest they be discouraged. In order to do this, parents must learn to control themselves; they themselves must know the discipline and teaching of the Lord. This is what Paul shows us.

New believers, especially parents and future parents, should know that even as it is not easy to be a husband or a wife, it is even harder to be a father or a mother. To be a husband or a wife is mostly one's own concern; to be a parent affects others. A husband or a wife only touches his or her mate's personal happiness, but a parent influences the happiness of the next generation. The future of the children depends upon the parents. Therefore, the responsibility of parents is great. God has delivered our children's bodies, souls, thoughts, lives, and futures into our hands. No person can influence another's destiny more than parents can their children's. They can almost direct their children to heaven or to hell. How tremendously important their responsibility is. They must learn how to be good parents as well as how to be good husbands and wives. Their responsibility as parents probably is more serious than their responsibility as husbands and wives.

Let us fellowship a little on how to be a Christian parent.

Sanctify Yourself

All who are parents ought to sanctify themselves before God for the sake of their children.

1. THE LORD SANCTIFIED HIMSELF

What does it mean to be sanctified before God? The Lord Jesus sanctified Himself for our sake. This does not refer to holiness by itself but to separation. The Lord Jesus was holy and His nature was holy. But for the sake of the church He further sanctified Himself. This means that though He could have done many things without compromising His own holy nature, He yet refused to do them for the sake of the weaknesses of His disciples. The disciples' weaknesses controlled the Lord and restricted His freedom in many ways. He was free Himself to do many things, but for fear that His disciples would misunderstand and be stumbled He refrained from doing them. So far as His nature was concerned He could have freely done them, but for the sake of the disciples He did not do them.

2. YOU SHOULD SANCTIFY YOURSELF

In like manner, all parents should sanctify themselves for their children's sake. This means that though they are free to do many things, for the sake of their children they will not. There are many words they no longer feel free to utter because of their children. From the day a child comes into the family, the parents need to sanctify themselves.

If you cannot control yourself, how can you control your children? If you cannot govern yourself, how can you govern your children? A person without children only hurts himself by his lack of control, but one who has children destroys his children as well as himself. Therefore, as soon as a Christian is entrusted with children, he must sanctify himself. For the rest of his life there are two or four or more pairs of eyes watching and watching. Even after he has left this world, those eyes will continue to remember what they have seen.

3. Live According to a High Standard

On the day your child is born, you should consecrate yourself to the Lord. You should set a moral standard for yourself—standards to govern your conduct at home, your manner, your judgment, your ideal, and your spiritual life. You must follow these standards strictly or else you may ruin your child as well as yourself. Many children are ruined by their own parents, parents who lack a moral standard, having neither ideals nor spiritual criteria.

I hope you will see that the way a child evaluates and judges things in the future is learned at his parent's knees. He may or may not hear what you tell him, but he will never forget what he has seen. He has learned from you.

Once they have children, parents should remember that all their ways will thereafter be continued in their children. Before you have a child, you may work or play according to your mood. But after the children come, you are restricted. Whether you feel elated or dejected, you still must follow the highest standard, for the future of your children much depends upon you, their Christian parent.

I recall that a brother once said, when his son got into trouble, "He is I, and I am he." Such a statement is absolutely correct. Many times parents can see themselves in their children when the children are in trouble. The children are merely a reflection of the parents.

I wish to say to all new believers that whenever they have children, they should rededicate themselves to God. They should commit the soul, life, and future of their children to the Lord, and henceforth they should be faithful in this stewardship. Many other kinds of work may be carried out within a one or two year period, but the work of parenthood is for life. It has no time limitation.

4. DEVELOP A SENSE OF STEWARDSHIP OVER YOUR CHILDREN

Neither failure in work nor failure in marriage can be compared with failure in parenthood. Why? Because when one is already grown up, he is well able to protect himself. But the child who is committed to you cannot protect himself. Could you go to the Lord and say, "You entrusted me with five children, and I lost three of them," or, "You trusted me with ten and I lost eight of them"? The church cannot be strong if this sense of stewardship is missing. How can the gospel be spread over the earth if you lose those born to you and then have to try to recover them from the world? You should at least bring your own children to the Lord. For you to not nurture them in the chastening and admonition of the Lord is wrong. Remember, it is the responsibility of the parents to bring up their children in the Lord.

Forgive me for saying this for it is my own word, but the worst failure in the church is the parents. No one is in a position to control parents. The children cannot. If you treat yourself indulgently, you will also treat your children loosely. How important for the parents to have self-control; how necessary for them to give up their own freedom. Otherwise, how can they stand before their God and give account for the souls entrusted to them?

Walk with God

All parents not only must recognize their responsibility and sanctify themselves for the children's sake but they also should learn to walk with God.

1. BE HOLY IN YOUR LIFE

It is true that one must sanctify himself for the sake of the children, but this does not suggest that one does it only for the children's sake. The Lord Jesus was holy, and He sanctified Himself for the disciples' sake. Even before He sanctified Himself for the sake of His disciples, He already was holy. Likewise, parents who sanctify themselves for the children's sake should at all times walk with God.

However zealous you may appear, your children will quickly see through you if you are not really zealous. You may deceive yourself but not them. How easily they penetrate your pretension if you are careful only before them and not when you are alone. For this reason, you must not only sanctify yourself before your children and for their sake, but you must also be truly holy and separated from the world. You must walk with God as Enoch of old did.

2. ENOCH WALKED WITH GOD AFTER HIS SON WAS BORN

"And Enoch lived sixty and five years, and begat Methuselah; and Enoch walked with God after he begat Methuselah three hundred years, and begat sons and daughters" (Gen. 5:21-22). We do not know anything about Enoch before he was sixty-five years old, but after he begat Methuselah we know he walked with God three hundred years before he was taken up.

This record in the Old Testament is quite special. When the burden of having a family came upon Enoch, he became aware of his unfitness. He felt the responsibility was too heavy for him, so he started to walk with God. The record does not say that he walked with God only in the presence of his son, for he himself was walking with God. He was convinced that unless he walked with God, he could not lead his son. Enoch begat many sons and daughters during those three hundred years, but meanwhile he continued to walk with God. Parenthood itself does not hinder people from walking with God; on the contrary, it constrains them to walk with Him and so be raptured. Remember that the first one raptured was a father. The raptured man had many children, yet he walked with God. The bearing of family responsibility reveals one's spiritual condition before God.

3. Do Not Have a Double Standard

To lead your children to God, you must yourself walk with God. Do not fancy that by pointing your finger towards heaven you may lead them to heaven. You yourself must walk ahead and let them follow. The reason for the failure of many Christian families is that the parents expect their children to be better than they are. They expect their children not to love the world and to go on with the Lord while they themselves stay behind. Such an expectation is futile. It is important that the parents have the same standard as the children. You cannot set up a standard for them and not live by it yourself. The standard which you follow in spiritual things will eventually be the standard of your children.

I once visited a family and witnessed the beating of a child by his mother because he had lied. As a matter of fact, though, both the father and the mother of this family told lies. Many times I found out they were liars. But the child was beaten for this very thing. The real issue, then, was not the child's telling a lie but rather in being found out in it. His lying technique was faulty. The actual problem in that house was whether or not a lie was discovered. If it were discovered, the boy would be punished. How can you help your children if you adopt such a double standard? Can you ask your children not to lie when you yourself do it? What is the use of asking them?

Nothing will ever be accomplished if you live by one standard and yet give your children another. What the children see in you is what they will accept. If they see a lie and not honesty, then the more you beat them, the worse they will become. It is like fathers telling their children they will be allowed to smoke after they reach eighteen. Children in a household where lies are told will imagine that when they are eighteen they will be permitted to lie. They may not tell lies now, but wait until they are eighteen. Then they will be free to lie. To act this way is to push your children into the world. You can only lead your children as Enoch led his if you walk with God as Enoch did. You cannot so lead them if you yourself do not walk that way.

Remember, your children will naturally learn to love what you love and hate what you hate. They will treasure what you treasure and condemn what you condemn. You must therefore set up one moral standard for both you and your children. Whatever your moral standard is, that will spontaneously be theirs. The standard of what it means to love the Lord will naturally become their standard of love to Him. There can be only one standard, not two, in the family.

I knew of one family where the father was a nominal Christian. He never went to church, but he wanted his children to go to church every Sunday. So every Sunday morning he would give his children some money for the offering. Then he would start to play cards with his three friends. Consequently, his children would spend the money he gave them on a snack, slip into the church at the time the pastor gave his text so as to report back to their father, and slide out to play afterwards. Thus, they could eat and play and report. This, of course, was an extreme case.

So, I hope you will see that when God entrusts you with children, you must have only one standard in the family. And once a standard is set, you must always maintain it. Remember, your children are watching. They are not listening to what you say, but they are watching what you do. They know wherein you are pretending. You cannot deceive them, for they know what your attitude is and what the fact is.

How very beautiful is the picture of Enoch walking with God for three hundred years after he begat Methuselah. He begat many sons and daughters and yet he still walked with God. Here was a true father, a man without pretense, and perfect in the sight of God.

Parents Must Be of One Mind

For a family to be solid, the Christian father and mother must be of one mind. For the sake of God, they must agree to sacrifice their own freedom and establish a strict moral standard. Neither the father nor the mother can have his or her special opinion.

Oftentimes the father and mother provide an opening for their children to sin because they themselves do not stand together. It is difficult for the children to follow a definite standard if the parents do not agree. If the father says yes and the mother says no (or vice versa), the children can choose to ask whoever is more lenient. This will further enlarge the gap between the father and the mother.

I knew an elderly couple who were both Christians. Each of them had his own ideas. As a result, they were good neither as husband and wife nor as parents. Their children would seek out the mother or the father according to their knowledge of who would approve a particular request. If the mother came home and asked why they had done a certain thing, they could answer that they had already asked the father. Sometimes it was the other way around. Thus the children played their game on the battlefield of the father and the mother and, in so doing, enjoyed tremendous freedom. Twenty years ago I told the parents that their children would not believe in the Lord if such a situation were prolonged. They disagreed with me then. Now their children are all grown up; some are in college and some are studying abroad, but none of them has believed in the Lord.

It is important for parents to be of one accord when a problem with the children arises. They need to present one mind to their children. No matter what the circumstance, you should first question the child who comes to you with a request as to whether he has asked mother and, if so, what did mother say. If you are the wife, then your first answer to the child must be, did he ask father and, if so, whatever father said is also what you say. Disregard the question of right or wrong on either the part of the father or of the mother; just simply maintain oneness. If there is a need for negotiation, do this privately between the two of you. Do not provide any loopholes for the children lest they end up doing whatever they please. Children are always looking for loopholes. You can and you must iron out your differences in private, but do not let the children find any loopholes between you. Then you can more easily bring your children to the Lord.

Respect the Child's Rights

A basic principle in the Bible concerning children is that they are given by the Lord. Hence, they are God's trust. Some day you will have to render account for this trust. You cannot say, "This child is mine," as if the child were exclusively yours, as if you have unlimited power over him till he becomes a man. Such a concept is heathen, not Christian. Christianity never recognizes children as one's private property. Rather, Christianity acknowledges them as a divine trust. It does not sanction despotic parental rule over the children until they reach the age of maturity.

1. PARENTAL AUTHORITY IS NOT UNLIMITED

Some people, after becoming Christians, still retain the concept that parents cannot be wrong. But, sad to say, the world has seen too many wrong parents. Frequently the parents are at fault. Let us not have a wrong idea about this and fancy that we have unlimited authority over our children.

Remember, you do not possess unlimited authority. Your child has a soul over which you do not have absolute control. His soul is subject to his own control. He may go to heaven or he may go to hell. This is his responsibility before God. You cannot treat him as a thing or as property. God has not given you unlimited authority over your child. He gives you unlimited authority over inanimate objects but not over souls. No one has absolute authority over another soul.

2. DO NOT VENT YOUR FRUSTRATIONS UPON YOUR CHILDREN

You communicate well with all kinds of people. You are reasonable with your friends, relatives, and colleagues. You are especially polite and respectful toward your boss. But, you treat your children as if they were your private possession. You forget that they have God-given souls. You discharge all your ill-temper on them. You treat them as you please. It seems you are courteous to everyone except your children. They are the ones upon whom you vent your wrath. I know some parents who are like that. They feel that they are not fully human if they are always courteous and gentle and never lose their temper. But how can they exhaust their bad temper? If they turn it on their colleagues, they will be neglected; if on their boss, they will be fired; if on their friends, they will be condemned. The only place they can afford to lose their temper without fear of reprisal is upon their children. Thus many parents have an awful temper toward their children.

Forgive me for speaking strongly. I have seen too many parents who on the one hand raved at their children and on the other hand turned to me and said, "Mr. Nee, this is a delicious dish. Please have some." How could I swallow the food? Those parents regarded their children as those on whom they could quite legitimately vent their wrath! Why did God give them children? That they should lose their temper? May God be merciful to us!

God never nullified all the privileges of a child. He did

not annul the child's self-respect or all of his freedom. He did not erase the child's independent personality when He placed him in your hand. You are not free to beat or scold as you please. Such a thought is definitely unchristian. Before God, the same standard of right and wrong applies to you as well as to your children. It must not be one standard for you and another for your children. Do you see this? I wish to tell new believers that they must be polite and gentle toward their children. They should not be rude or careless in their treatment of their children.

To be rude and careless to one's children only makes one more undisciplined. Every person growing in the Christian life must learn to control himself, especially in regard to his children. Such self-control stems from a respect for the child's soul. No matter how small or weak a child is, he has his individuality. God has given it to him and no one has the right to infringe upon it.

A child is a trust. His moral standard comes from your moral standard. Parents have no right to pour out their private frustrations on their children. It is wrong for Christians to lose their temper, and it is wrong to vent ill-temper on children. You should be reasonable even to your children. It must be nay, nay and yea, yea. The greatest coward in the world is he who oppresses the weak and small.

3. Do Not Become a Cross to Your Children

Two girls were studying in the same school. One of them once told her schoolmate, "If it were necessary, I know my father would die for me." Just by listening to that child's comment about her father, you know what kind of a Christian father he was. The other girl also came from a

Christian family. Her father was very strict and often got angry at his daughter thoughtlessly. One day at school she listened to a Christian message. After she went home, her father asked her what she had learned that day. She answered, "I know now that the Lord gave you to me to be my cross." Is this not a problem to many children, that they have to reckon that the Lord gave their fathers or mothers to them to be their crosses? In this particular story, both the fathers were Christians. Yet, what a difference!

Tell parents to be slow in demanding obedience from their children. Ask them first to be good parents before God. How can anyone be a good Christian if he or she is not a good parent? God has given children to the parents but not for them to be crosses to the children. Parents ought to learn to respect the freedom, the individuality, and the souls of their children.

Do Not Provoke Your Children to Wrath

Paul shows us that it is of utmost importance that parents not provoke their children to wrath.

1. USE AUTHORITY WITH RESTRAINT

What is meant by provoking the children to wrath? It means the excessive use of your authority, overpowering your children with your strength, financial or physical or whatever. In every way you are stronger than your child. You may overwhelm him with your monetary strength if you threaten: "If you don't listen to me, I won't give you any money," or, "If you don't listen, I won't give you food or clothing." Since you support him, you can oppress him by withdrawing financial support. Or you may simply subdue him by your physical strength or perhaps by your overbearing will. You provoke him to wrath. You press him to such an extent that he just waits for the day of liberation. When that day comes, he will throw off all restraint and claim freedom in everything.

I know of a brother whose father gambled, smoked at home, and even embezzled public funds—but went to church on Sunday. He even forced all his children to go to church or else they would be severely punished. This brother later testified that during that time he vowed he would never enter a church once he could support himself. Thank God, he was saved. Otherwise, he would be another person who was fiercely antichristian. Such a thing is truly most serious. One cannot himself be unattractive yet force his children to go to church. It will only provoke them to wrath. Parents should not use their authority excessively lest they provoke their children. They must not cause their children to be hardened.

One person I used to know is yet unsaved though as a child he was forced to read the Bible at home and in school, for it was a mission school. I do not say parents should not persuade their children to read the Bible. I do say, however, that they themselves must be attractive to their children. How can you show them the preciousness of the Lord if all you do is force them? The mother of this boy was herself only a nominal Christian. She had a terrible temper; yet she compelled her son to read the Bible and to attend mission school. One day her son asked her when he could stop reading the Bible. She answered that he might stop reading it after he graduated from high school. So, as soon as he got his high school diploma, he took his three copies of the Bible to the backyard and burned them.

Therefore, do not provoke your children to wrath. You must learn to show love and gentleness to them. You need to have a good testimony before them and be attractive to them. Use your authority with restraint, for excessive use of authority may stiffen resistance.

2. SHOW APPRECIATION TO THE CHILDREN

When the children do well, parents should show proper appreciation. Some parents only seem to know to beat and to scold. This easily provokes the children and discourages even those who really have a desire to be good. Paul says, "Provoke not your children, that they be not discouraged." Children should be encouraged when they do well. They need to be rewarded as well as disciplined. Otherwise, they will be disheartened.

I once read a story about a little girl whose mother only knew how to scold. This child, though, had a good nature. She felt that her mother was not kind to her, so one day she tried especially hard to please the mother. In the evening, the mother undressed her and started to leave. She called her mother back but she would not answer when her mother asked why she had called. So her mother started to leave again, but again she called her mother back. When she was again asked why, she said, "Mother, don't you have something to say?" When the mother again left, having nothing to say, the little girl cried for two hours. How insensitive the mother was, so void of feeling that she knew nothing but beating and scolding.

There are more passages in the New Testament for parents than for children. This is because when parents do wrong, only the Lord teaches them; but when children are wrong, the whole world judges. The Bible definitely tells us that due to lack of sensitivity, parents can really provoke their children to wrath and discouragement. The occupation of being a parent is harder than any other occupation. It requires the utmost concentration. Therefore, do not be insensitive.

Speak Accurately

Parents' words to their children are highly effective. Their words are as important as their examples.

1. Do Not Make Empty Promises

Do not say something to the children that you cannot fulfill. Never make an empty promise to them. If you do not have the power to realize a promise, do not promise. If your child asks you to buy something, consider carefully before you promise. Every word you say must be dependable. Do not treat this matter of accuracy as a small thing. Never let your children doubt your words. They must believe that your words are trustworthy. If the children discover a lack of trustworthiness in their parents' words, they themselves will be careless in everything when they grow up. They will surmise that they can say things and do things thoughtlessly. Parents should not try to be diplomatic or tactful if such words are not factual. Many parents are too good: they promise everything the children ask for, but only fulfill a few of the promises. Such empty words only disappoint the children. You should say "yes" to what you can do, "no" to what you cannot do, and "maybe" to what you are not sure of. Let your words be accurate.

2. Enforce Your Orders

Sometimes it is not promises that are overused but orders. Whenever you ask your children to do something, you must see that it is carried out; otherwise, do not open your mouth. You should make them believe that your words represent your will. If you have given them an order, do not forget it or compromise it by relegating it to next time. Show your children, whether it be an order or a promise, that words are sacred. For example, as soon as you tell your child to sweep his room every morning, your strength is put to the test. If he fails to do it, he must be ordered to do it the second morning. If he does not do it this year, he must still be asked to do it next year. He must be convinced that his father does not speak casually, that whatever his father says must be done. Should he discover that you do not mean business in your words, your words will immediately lose their value. Hence, all that you say must be substantiated, must be enforced.

3. CORRECT YOUR INACCURACIES

Whenever you have spoken with exaggeration, you must find opportunity to correct it before your children. Your words need to be accurate. Perhaps you exaggerate three cows for two cows or eight birds for five birds. Learn to correct these figures before your children, showing them the sacredness of words. Everything in family life must establish good Christian character. So, you need to affirm the sacredness of words; you need to lead the children to understand this sacredness. If you say something inaccurately, confess it with all seriousness. Set a good example in the family so your children will know the sanctity of words.

Difficulties in accuracy of words stem from a lack of the admonition of the Lord. Parents must not only give their children the admonition of the Lord but also should exemplify such teaching. They should show their children how sacred words are. Promises must be kept, orders must be real, and words must be accurate. Thus their children will receive some spiritual education.

Nurture Your Children in the Chastening and Admonition of the Lord

What is meant by the admonition of the Lord? It means instruction on how one should behave. In so instructing your children, you must treat them as Christians, not as unbelievers. The Lord wants you to expect your children to become Christians; hence you must treat them as such. You should instruct them according to the norm of a good Christian.

1. CHANNEL CHILDREN'S AMBITION

A great problem with children is ambition. Every child has his ambition. If children could print their name cards, many of them would write such titles as "The Future President," "The Future Chairman," or, "The Future Queen." If you are worldly, your children will naturally think of being a president, a millionaire, or a great educator. Whatever your world is, that will be your children's ambition. Because of this, parents must try to correct and channel their children's ambition. You yourself must be a lover of the Lord, not a lover of the world. Instill in their young hearts the understanding that to suffer for the Lord is noble and to be a martyr is glorious. You yourself need to set an example for them. You must often tell them what your ambition is. Tell them what kind of Christian you want to be. In this way you can turn their ambition to that which is noble and glorious.

2. Do Not Encourage Children's Pride

Besides outward ambition, children also have the problem of inward pride. They like to boast of their cleverness, talent, or eloquence. Usually a child can find many things to brag about, imagining himself to be someone very special. Parents should not stifle their children, neither should they nurture their pride. Many parents educate their children in a wrong way by encouraging their vanity. When people praise your child before him, you may tell him that there are many other children like him in the world. Do not encourage his pride, but instruct him according to the chastening and admonition of the Lord. Do not let him lose his self-respect, but also do not allow him to be proud. You should not break down his self-respect, but you must show him wherein he has overestimated himself. Sometimes it takes young people ten to twenty years of social grinding before they start to do well. This is a waste of much precious time, all because they have been so proud and indulgent at home that they cannot humble themselves enough to really do any work well.

3. Teach Children to Accept Defeat and to Learn Humility

A Christian must learn how to admire others even when defeated by them. It is easier to behave well in victory but harder to behave well in defeat. There may yet be some people who are humble in victory, but few are those who do not speak unkindly of others in defeat. The Christian attitude is to be humble in strength and to accept defeat with good will. Children like to win. Such a desire is good; it helps them to excel in sports and in studies. Your child should study well at school, but you also must teach and encourage him to be humble. Tell him that there may be many other students better than he is. Also teach him how to accept defeat in good spirit. This is a difficulty with children. For example, if two play ball, the winner may be inflated, while the loser may either accuse the referee of being unfair or blame the sun shining into his eyes. Remember, therefore, to encourage a humble attitude in your children. Train them to develop their character. They should learn how to win and how to prefer others over themselves in defeat. Let us nurture them in the discipline and instruction of the Lord.

It is natural for children to unjustly say that the student who does well in examinations is favored by the teacher whereas their own failure is because the teacher does not like them. Here you see the need for humility. Christians must learn the virtue of accepting defeat. If other people excel, acknowledge it openly. Accept defeat by saying that the victor is more clever, more diligent, better than we are. It is unchristian to be puffed up in victory. It is a Christian virtue to acknowledge defeat in a good spirit. In the family, children should be taught to recognize those who are stronger than they. This will help them to know themselves better after they become Christians. A Christian ought to be able to praise those who are better than he is as well as to know what he himself is. Children who are trained in this way are more open to spiritual things.

4. Teach Children How to Choose

Give children the opportunity to make choices when they are still young. Do not always make decisions for them in everything until they are eighteen or twenty, and then suddenly thrust them into the world. If you do that, they will not know how to choose for themselves. So, in bringing up your children, give them ample opportunity to choose. Let them express what they like or dislike. Show them whether what they like is the right thing or not. Help them to choose rightly. Some children like to be dressed in one color while some others prefer another. Let them have their choice.

If children are not given the opportunity to choose, they will not be able, when they reach the age of marriage, to rule in their families. Give your children as much opportunity as possible to choose; also, you should instruct them about their choice.

5. TEACH CHILDREN HOW TO TAKE CARE OF THINGS

You must teach your children how to take care of things. Give them opportunity to manage their own shoes, stockings, rooms, and so forth. Give them a little instruction and then ask them to do it by themselves. Thus they will learn how to take care of things from their youth. Some children never had the opportunity to start their lives right, for their fathers loved so blindly as to have completely spoiled them. But a Christian must help his children to manage their own affairs.

I trust, if the Lord be gracious to the church, half of the people added to it will be the children of Christian parents, the other half will be rescued from the world. A church cannot be strong if the increase comes only from the world and not from the children of Christian parents. In Paul's generation, when the church was just starting, people were saved directly from the world; but the next generation, like Timothy, more often came from the family. We cannot expect people always to come into the church directly from the world. We should hope to see people coming in from Christian families. The gospel of God does indeed rescue people from the world. In addition, though, people such as Timothy must yet be brought in through the chastening and admonition of the Lord administered by grandmother Lois and mother Eunice. Only thus will the church be enriched. You must arrange to have your children manage their own things. Hold family meetings and let them learn how to take care of things. Both the boys and the girls need to be taught so that later on they can be good husbands and good wives.

What is the situation today? Many boys and girls who ought to have been nurtured in the discipline and instruction of the Lord by their parents have to be taken care of by the church. Because the parents do not live as good Christians, the church is compelled to preach the gospel and save those children back from the world. Had the Christian parents fulfilled their responsibility, these children would be brought in without creating any problem for the church. The church would be relieved of half its burden.

Lead Your Children to the Lord

One way of leading children to the Lord is an effective family altar. In the Old Testament the tent and the altar were joined together. In other words, the family and consecration are connected; united family prayer and reading the Bible together are indispensable.

1. HAVE FAMILY WORSHIP ON THE CHILDREN'S LEVEL

Some so-called family worship is a failure, either because it is too long or too deep. The children sit through without knowing what it is all about. I am opposed to families inviting us to preach deeper truth to them with the children sitting there. Sometimes a family gathering continues for an hour or two and what is considered is all deeper truth. This is really a hardship on the children. And sometimes parents are not sensitive to it at all. In a family gathering, the children must be the first consideration. The gathering is not for you, because you can worship in the church. Never force your level on the family gathering. All that you do in the family must be on the level of the children and best suited to their taste.

2. Encourage and Attract the Children

Another difficulty in a family gathering is the lack of love. The children are not drawn to the gathering by the father or the mother but by the whip. They do not want to attend; they only come out of fear of the whip. This will never do. Try to attract them, not to whip them. Think of ways to encourage them. I hope new believers will never beat their children because they fail to attend family devotions. You may whip them but once; yet the adverse effect may be for life. So in the family gathering, you who are parents must try to attract your children. Never force them to attend.

3. Hold Family Worship Twice Daily

We suggest having family devotions twice a day, once in the morning and once in the evening. One way would be to let the father lead in the morning and the mother in the evening. The parents will need to rise earlier in the morning so there will be time for devotions after breakfast before the children go to school. The time must not be long, not longer than fifteen minutes. Ask each of them to

94

read a verse. The father may pick out a few words and explain them. If possible, get the children to memorize part of the verse. Then close the time with a prayer by either the father or the mother. Ask God to bless them. Do not pray for things too deep for them to comprehend. Do not pray too long. Pray simply and in a way the children can understand.

The evening time can be a little longer. Let the mother lead. There is no need to read the Bible but prayer is absolutely a necessity. The mother especially should gather her children around her and talk to them. The father may sit by the side. Mother may try to draw out the children and get them to talk. Let them tell if they have had any problems during the day, or if they have had a fight, or if there is something on their hearts which makes them uneasy. Something is drastically wrong if a mother is unable to get her children to talk. It is a failure on the part of the mother if there is a distance between her and her children. The mother ought to be the confidante of her children. Try to draw them out. Let them pray a little. Teach them a few words. Such a time must be living. Lead them to confess, but do not force them. Be very natural and avoid all pretension. Let the children be spontaneous. If there is anything to confess, confess; if not, leave it. The hypocrisy of many children is formed by severe parents. They do not want to lie, but they are forced to by their parents. Conclude the evening time with a short prayer lest the children grow weary.

Parents must lead the children in all simplicity. Pray for them continually until each child knows how to pray.

4. Lead the Children to Repentance

You need to show your children what sin is. Notice if they are repentant. Bring them to the Lord. When the time is ripe, help them to accept the Lord in a definite way. Then take them to the church that they may have a part in the life of the church. In this way you will lead your children to the true knowledge of God.

Encourage a Loving Family Atmosphere

A family atmosphere is a loving atmosphere. Lack of communication in the family is due to a lack of love.

The future condition of the children depends largely on the family atmosphere. If the children do not have the nourishment of love while they are small, they will soon develop a hard, solitary, rebellious attitude. Many people cannot associate with others because as children they did not have love in their families. If the family has frequent strifes and quarrels, the children do not grow up normally. They naturally become withdrawn. They look down on people because they have an inferiority complex. Those who have an inferiority complex strive to exalt themselves in order to be equal with others.

Many of the hard-boiled elements in society—such as bandits and rebels—have never experienced love in their families. As a result, their human nature has undergone a change; they have become abnormal. When such people are brought into the church, lots of adjustments will have to be made. I often feel that half the work of the church ought to have been done by good parents. Due to the parents' failure, a heavy burden falls upon the church. To avoid this, new believers need to be instructed to treat their children well. There must be joy, gentleness, and love in the family. Such a family produces normal children.

The parents should learn to be friends to their children. Do not allow your children to become strangers to you.

Remember, friendship is cultivated, not inherited. Learn to be close to your children, always glad to help, so that when they have trouble, they will tell you; when they are weak, they will seek your help. Do not let them seek out other people when they need help. Make it possible for them to come to you in success as well as in failure. A friend is one who is easy to approach and to talk to. Be like a friend to your children. Do not sit on the throne and judge, but try to help them in their weakness. Sit down with them and discuss their problem together. Let them seek you out as they would seek out their friends. If the parents can be friends to their children, they are good parents.

Cultivate this friendship when your children are small. Let me tell you frankly, the closeness and intimacy of your children to you depends upon the way you treat them during the first twenty years. It is impossible that your children be distant from you during the first twenty years and then be close to you after that. As the years go by, if there is distance, it usually grows greater. Many children have no admiration for their parents and no friendship with them. When they are in trouble, they go to their parents as going to a judge. This ought not be your case. When your children have trouble, you must be the first one they seek to unburden themselves to. Families like this have few problems and those that they do have can all be solved.

Discipline Your Children Wisely

When children do wrong, they should be disciplined. It is not right not to chasten a child.

1. BE AFRAID OF DISCIPLINING UNWISELY

Chastening, however, is very difficult. Parents ought to be afraid of whipping their children even as they would be afraid of whipping their own parents. No child may beat his parents. Yet it would be easier for one's parents to forgive such a beating than it would be for one's children to forgive. Learn, therefore, to be afraid of whipping your children.

2. USE THE ROD WHEN NECESSARY

Children must be chastened, though. "He that spareth his rod hateth his son; but he that loveth him chasteneth him betimes" (Prov. 13:24).

This is the wisdom of Solomon. Parents must learn to use the rod, for it is necessary.

3. CHASTEN JUSTLY

However, chastening must be done justly. Never whip your child because you have lost your temper or when you are out of sorts. If you whip in anger, you yourself are wrong. You are not qualified to chasten your child. You need to have your wrath calmed down before God.

4. SHOW THE CHILDREN THEIR FAULT

In some cases, whipping is necessary. But you must show your child why he deserves it. Doubtless he is in need of chastening, yet he also has the need of being shown his fault. Each time you chasten a child, tell him wherein he was wrong.

5. CONSIDER BEATING AS A BIG THING

Do not make whipping a common thing. Look upon it

as a big affair. Call the whole family together and let all know about it. For the father or the mother to whip a child is like a surgeon operating on a patient. It is not because of being provoked to anger, but because the cutting is necessary in order to deal with the difficulty. Likewise, in disciplining, the parent must be absolutely calm. No parent should beat the child when he himself is angry.

How should it be done? I have a suggestion to make: when a child has made a very serious mistake that requires a whipping, you may ask his brother to prepare a basin of cold water and his sister to be ready with a towel. Then you should show your child wherein he is wrong and that a wrong must be seriously punished. Tell him that to flee from chastisement is also wrong. People who have the courage to sin ought to have the courage to accept punishment. After you have explained this to him, you may strike his hand twice or thrice. This may bruise his hand and cause it to swell. Call his brother to help soak his hand in the cold water to keep the swelling down. Then ask his sister to gently dry his hand with the towel. The whole act is like going through a ritual. This will show them that there is only love, no hate, in the family.

Many chastenings today are indications of anger or hate, not of love. You say you love your children, but who can believe you? I cannot. You must show your children wherein they are wrong. You must let them know that you nurse no hatred in beating them. If the case is too serious, then either the father or the mother may take some of the whipping for them. This will impress them with the seriousness of the case. It will help them to remember throughout their lives so that they will not heedlessly sin.

Such, then, is the admonition of the Lord, not the admonition of your temper. It is the chastening of the

Lord, not the chastening of your wrath. I am against parents losing their tempers. The ill-temper of the parents can damage the future of the children. In a Christian family, the parents must learn to love as well as to chasten.

Great Children Come from Great Parents

Finally, I want to say that many of God's great servants have come from great parents. Since the day of Timothy, many of those used by God have descended from great parents. John Wesley was one; John Newton was another; John G. Paton, one of the most illustrious missionaries in the world, was a third. Very few fathers were like John Paton's father. When John was of an advanced age, he was still telling how, whenever he was tempted to sin, he remembered his father and his father's prayers for him. John came from a poor family. There was only one bedroom, one kitchen, and one small room. Whenever he heard his father praying and sighing in that small room, he trembled. He knew his father was agonizing for the children's souls. Even as a grown man, John could yet remember his father's sigh. How he thanked God for giving him such a father that he might not sin. Had he sinned, he would offend not only the Father who was in heaven but also the father who was on earth. Rarely was there a father like John's, and rarely was there such a great son like John.

If, in our generation, parents learn to be good parents, how many strong and vigorous brothers and sisters we will have in the next generation. Frequently I feel constrained to say that the future of the church depends upon the parents. There need to be people God can raise up when

He desires to bless His church. There need to be more Timothys, so that He will not have to bring people out from the world but He will be able to bring in those who come from Christian families.

FRIENDSHIP

Ye adulteresses, know ye not that the friendship of the world is enmity with God? Whosoever therefore would be a friend of the world maketh himself an enemy of God.

James 4:4

Be not unequally yoked with unbelievers: for what fellowship have righteousness and iniquity? or what communion hath light with darkness? And what concord hath Christ with Belial? or what portion hath a believer with an unbeliever? And what agreement hath a temple of God with idols? for we are a temple of the living God; even as God said, I will dwell in them, and walk in them; and I will be their God, and they shall be my people. Wherefore, come ye out from among them, and be ye separate, saith the Lord, and touch no unclean thing; and I will receive you, and will be to you a Father, and ye shall be to me sons and daughters, saith the Lord Almighty.

2 Cor. 6:14–18

Blessed is the man that walketh not in the counsel of the wicked, nor standeth in the way of sinners, nor sitteth in the seat of scoffers: but his delight is in the law of Jehovah; and on his law doth he meditate day and night. And he shall be like a tree planted by the streams of water, that bringeth forth its fruit in its season, whose leaf also doth not wither; and whatsoever he doeth shall prosper. The wicked are not so, but are like the chaff which the wind driveth away. Therefore the wicked shall not stand in the judgment, nor sinners in the congregation of the righteous. For Jehovah knoweth the way of the righteous; but the way of the wicked shall perish.

Ps. 1

Friendship Not Emphasized in the Bible

It is rather special that the Bible hardly mentions the matter of friends in relation to God's children, though the word "friend" occurs many times. It is found in Genesis and Proverbs and in Matthew and Luke. Most of these times it refers to people outside of Christ. Rarely is it used of friends in the Lord. If I remember correctly, the word "friends" is used only twice in reference to Paul, both times being in Acts. Once was when ". . . certain also of the Asiarchs, being his [Paul's] friends, sent unto him and besought him not to adventure himself into the theatre" in Ephesus (Acts 19:31). Again, on the way to Rome, ". . . Julius treated Paul kindly, and gave him leave to go unto his friends and refresh himself" (Acts 27:3). In a third New Testament reference, John wrote, "The friends salute thee. Salute the friends by name" (3 John 14). The fact that there are so few references to Christian friends indicates that the Bible does not stress this matter.

Why is it that friendship is not emphasized in the Bible? It is because the Word of God emphasizes another relationship, that of brothers and sisters. How to be brothers and sisters in the Lord is of basic and primary importance. This is what needs to be strengthened, not the matter of friendship.

Meaning of Friendship

1. BASED ON LOVE

What does being a friend mean, especially in relationships between believers? Friendship can exist between old and young, husband and wife, father and son, brother and brother, or sister and sister. To be friends means to be able to love and to fellowship with each other. It transcends natural relationships.

Many human relationships are based on marriage, or blood relationships. Friendship, however, sets these aside and speaks only of love. Friendship is something that may be added to the relationship of husband and wife, of father and son, of mother and daughter, or of teacher and pupil. Also, people of the same social standing, same age, and same pursuit may have friendly relationships.

2. AN IMPORTANT WORLDLY SYSTEM

Before believing in the Lord Jesus, before accepting Him as Savior, there is no brother-sister relationship in the Lord. Hence, to the unbelievers of the world, friendship becomes most important. However, for us this is no longer so. That is why friendship is rarely mentioned in the New Testament epistles; its importance has been greatly diminished in the lives of the children of God.

Man is not so constituted that he can be fully satisfied by family relationships or mere social contacts. He needs friends to meet his inward longing, for friendship is established not on blood but on love. Many of our relationships are entered into by reason of birth, but the relationship of friends is of self-choice. Hence, friendship becomes a foremost matter before we believe in the Lord. Everyone needs friends—three, five, eight, ten. Those who

DO ALL TO THE GLORY OF GOD

are highly sociable may have hundreds of friends. Such friends may be quite intimately related and may communicate with one another in love. Indeed, before we become Christians, friends occupy a significant place in our lives.

If a person has no friends, others will think something must be wrong with him. It must be that he has an abnormal or peculiar temperament or that he is of an undependable character. Ordinarily, a person must have some friends.

Friendships in the World Terminated

As soon as one believes in the Lord Jesus, he is charged by God to desist from his former friendships.

deep seated hatred.

1. ENMITY WITH GOD

"Friendship of the world is enmity with God" (James 4:4). The "world" here may mean "the people of the world." If we would be friends with the people of the world because we love the world, then we make ourselves enemies of God. "If any man love the world, the love of the Father is not in him" (1 John 2:15).

Tell new believers emphatically that after they become Christians, one of the first things they must do is change their friends completely. (There are quite a few "first things" for new believers in these *Basic Lessons*.) I used to tell new believers, "Now that you have believed in the Lord, you need to change your friends completely, make a complete change just as you would of your clothing and other things." I know what I am talking about. If a new believer does not change his friends, his spiritual future is bound to be shallow and weak. As soon as one believes in the Lord, he must free himself of his former friendships. It

106

FRIENDSHIP

is wonderful to know that as love of the Lord enters, love of man exits. When the life of the Lord is put in us, it becomes impossible for us to befriend the world.

Let us note, though, that our Lord has not said that we must be hostile to the world in order to love Him. It does not mean that we must not even nod our heads when we meet people on the street. "Friendship with the world is enmity with God" does not suggest that we should treat the people of the world as enemies. It only means that former deep friendships and intimate relationships can no longer exist. You may still love a former friend, but your aim is to get him saved. You may yet befriend him, but your purpose is to invite him to hear the gospel. This is what Cornelius did in inviting two classes of people to his home to hear Peter. One class was his relatives, and the other class included close friends. You too bring your relatives and close friends to hear the gospel. Your aim is not to maintain the former relationships but rather to bring them to the Lord. Once you know a person, you cannot stop knowing him. One who has been a friend is still a friend. How can you cut off all communication after being friends for years? So what we really mean here is that once we experience the change of coming to the Lord, former relationships simply do not exist. Hereafter when we see our former friends, we still talk with them, and when they have a problem, we yet converse with them. But we have received a new life while they have not, and this is a line of demarcation which cannot be violated.

In traveling or in racing, the lighter the weight the better. In spiritual things, more dealings with sins will reduce the weight; more restitutions will also lessen the burden. To be separated from some of the old friends will lighten the load too, but adding on more friends will

107

eventually crush the runner. I see many brothers and sisters loaded down with friends. They are not able to run well in the course which God has laid before them. Unbelievers have a different moral standard; though they may not drag you down, they will not pull you up either.

2. UNEQUAL YOKING

"Be not unequally yoked with unbelievers" (2 Cor. 6:14). Many people seem to think this refers exclusively to marriage. I believe it does include marriage, but more than that too. It comprises all kinds of friendships and relationships between believers and unbelievers. Here we are shown the utter incompatibility of believers and unbelievers.

THE MEANING OF AN UNEQUAL YOKE

"Be not unequally yoked with unbelievers" is a general statement followed by a colon in Scripture. To find out what the statement means, read the five questions that follow: "For what fellowship have righteousness and iniquity? or what communion hath light with darkness? And what concord hath Christ with Belial? or what portion hath a believer with an unbeliever? And what agreement hath a temple of God with idols? for we are a temple of the living God; even as God said, I will dwell in them, and walk in them; and I will be their God, and they shall be my people" (2 Cor. 6:14–16). These five questions tell us how it is unequal for believers and unbelievers to bear one yoke.

To be unequally yoked is not a blessing but a sorrow. I hope Christians will see that we must not maintain an intimate relationship with unbelievers, whether in the sphere of society, business, friendship, or marriage. Believers have one standard and unbelievers another. Believers have the teaching of faith, but unbelievers follow their doctrine of unbelief. Believers possess a believing viewpoint, and unbelievers hold on to an unbelieving viewpoint. When you try to bring these together, the result is not blessing but pain. Their viewpoints, opinions, moral standards, and judgments are so different from ours that there is a tugging in two directions. To put these two under one yoke will either break the yoke or cause the believer to follow the unbeliever.

I wish all new believers would understand that to be friends with unbelievers invariably results in loss. Do not think that you can pull up the unbeliever. To pull him up does not require your being his bosom friend. I have pulled up former friends without involving myself in intimate association with them. It is possible to pull them over without maintaining the old relationship. But if you continue the old friendships, you will eventually be pulled down by them.

C. H. Spurgeon gave a good illustration of this. The following story seems to me to be rather clever. Once a young woman came to see Spurgeon and asked him if she could be friends with an unbelieving young man. She said her aim was to lead him to Christ and so she had decided to be engaged to him fairly soon. Spurgeon then asked the young lady to climb up onto a high table. She could not but obey. Spurgeon, already quite advanced in age, told the girl to grasp his hand and try her best to pull him up onto the table. She tried, but of course she could not do it. Then Spurgeon said that he would pull her down. With just one pull, she came down. Spurgeon then said, "It is easy to be pulled down, but hard to pull up." Thus was this sister's question solved.

Tell your former friends that you have believed in the Lord Jesus. When you see them, bring them to the Lord. When I was younger, I had many friends in school. After I trusted in the Lord, whenever I visited my friends, I took my Bible with me and talked of the Lord. I confessed my inglorious past. Formerly I had gambled and had often been to the movies. My friends had easily persuaded me to do these things. But after I believed in the Lord, I would sit down with them and take out my Bible. Soon what had happened to me became generally known. From then on, my friends would not inform me when they went gambling or to the movies. It is better to be unwelcomed than to be pulled down by your former friends. To maintain some association is good, but do not crave for intimate friendship. Be polite and friendly but not deeply involved. You belong to the Lord, and you must bring the Lord to them.

If you faithfully serve the Lord and if you bring the Lord to these friends, sooner or later you will see them either turn to the Lord or forsake you. These are the two alternatives. Rarely is it any other way.

FIVE BIBLICAL QUESTIONS

First, "What fellowship have righteousness and iniquity?" Once you believe in the Lord, you begin to know what righteousness is. Several days ago a brother testified that he saw it was unrighteous to enter the public park with a borrowed season ticket. Believers need to be shown what is righteous and what is unrighteous. They must deal with past unrighteous deeds and old indebtednesses. The most moral people of the world still do not know what righteousness is. Righteousness and iniquity conflict, and there is no fellowship between them. Do you not realize that believers should not take advantage of others in even the smallest thing? Some people often like to take advantage of others. Certain things you once might have approved of, but now you feel they are unrighteous. So how can you again have fellowship with such unrighteousness? Your judgment now is so different from theirs. There is no possibility of fellowship unless you change righteousness into unrighteousness.

Second, "What communion hath light with darkness?" You have been enlightened and now you really see things in their true light. Your worldly friend, though, is in darkness and cannot see the true character of things. A child of God who has gone a long way in the Lord even finds it difficult to fellowship with a carnal Christian living in darkness. How much more impossible it is for an advanced Christian to commune with one who has never seen any light! Remember, the conflict involved is basic: there can be no communion between light and darkness. Those in darkness may do many things you cannot. Their philosophy, ethics, outlook, and life purpose are all different from yours. You are in the light; but they are in darkness. How can you commune with them, for there is a difference in nature?

Third, "What concord hath Christ with Belial?" Belial here points to Satan, for the word means "contemptibleness" or "wickedness." Satan is truly contemptible and wicked. We belong to Christ, while unbelievers are children of Belial. Through Christ we are noble in God's sight, but they are contemptible. We are bought with a price, yet not with corruptible gold and silver but with the precious blood of God's Son. There are many things we cannot do because it would violate our Christian position and dignity.

But these people belong to Belial. They may do many

111

things which we cannot. They can take advantage of others; they can seek their own profit at others' expense. But we Christians have a glory and position. How can the two concur? How can the two bear the same yoke? One will pull this direction and the other will pull that direction. Surely the yoke will break!

Fourth, "What portion hath a believer with an unbeliever?" Here is another distinct contrast. You are a man of faith but he has no faith. You believe but he does not believe. You know God by faith; he believes not and knows not God. You live by faith, so you can trust God; he has no faith, so he must look to himself. You testify that everything is in God's hand, but he says that all things are in his own hand. These are two disparate situations. What portion has a believer with an unbeliever? Believing God is as natural as breathing to you, but he finds it hard to believe for he does not even care to. He will ridicule you for being conservative, backward, foolish. How, then, can we have unbelieving friends? If we do, they will surely pull us down with them quickly.

Fifth, "What agreement hath a temple of God with idols?" Let us notice what is meant by the temple of God and what is meant by idols. I think this refers to the holiness of the physical body, for it is followed by "we are a temple of the living God." In 1 Corinthians we find the body is considered as the temple of God. Here is a people whose body is the temple of God; there is also another people who worship idols. You must not defile the temple of God. When you go out with your friends, they often do things which pertain to the body such as drinking and smoking. But your body is God's temple. You cannot corrupt or defile this temple. Hereafter you must keep your body as God's temple. The living God dwells in you;

do not defy Him. What agreement have we, the temple of God, with idols? Unbelievers are the temple of idols, for they are related to idols—either idols with or without form. They do not seek holiness of the body. But we do. Have we not seen how they are careless about their bodies? But we respect our body and we keep our bodies holy. It is impossible to make these two kinds of people agree.

Therefore, do not be intimate friends with unbelievers. If you do, there can be only one result: you will be pulled down. Do not boast that you are such a strong and steadfast person that it will not hurt to have a few unbelieving friends. Let me tell you, even if we have trusted in the Lord for many years, we should still be very much afraid to communicate with unbelieving friends. Such contacts can easily hurt our spiritual life. In seeking out unbelievers, you should aim either at taking them to meetings or at witnessing to them. Any other contact is highly dangerous. Once in their midst, you are prone to lower your standard. It is not easy to maintain a Christian standard among them.

3. The Influence of Bad Conversations

"Be not deceived: Evil companionships corrupt good morals" (1 Cor. 15:33). "Evil companionships" means improper communications, while "corrupt" carries the thought of wood being corrupted by worms.

BRINGS CORRUPTION

"Good morals" in a lighter vein is "good manners." Improper communications will corrupt your good appearance. At first you were pious before God, but, in the company of unbelieving friends, you begin to jest and laugh. Some of the jokes you ought not to laugh at, for they are unbecoming. But you set aside your self-control in their midst because you know they welcome looseness.

Evil communications corrupt good manners. These two are opposites. One is evil and the other is good. Evil corrupts good. It will corrupt the life of the Lord in believers. Believers ought to have good habits. They should spend time cultivating good habits before the Lord. They should learn to control themselves. They should gradually exercise themselves unto godliness.

RESTORATION TAKES TIME

Every time you have improper communications with unbelievers, you incur loss. It may take you three, four, or even five days to be restored to your original state, for those unbelievers may have influenced your good manners and affected your conduct.

4. NEITHER WALK, NOR STAND, NOR SIT

The psalmist says, "Blessed is the man that walketh not in the counsel of the wicked, nor standeth in the way of sinners, nor sitteth in the seat of scoffers: but his delight is in the law of Jehovah; and on his law doth he meditate day and night" (Ps. 1:1–2).

WALK NOT IN THE COUNSEL OF THE WICKED

Unbelievers have lots of counsel to give. It is most pitiful, though, for children of God, when faced with problems, to seek the counsel of unbelievers. Let me tell you that what they counsel is what you cannot do. I too have many unbelieving acquaintances. I know that such people often offer advice without your asking. As you listen to them, though, you know at once that their thoughts are focused on one thing: how to profit one's self. They do not ask if the thing is right or whether it is God's will. They have only one motive, and that is, personal profit. Can we follow the advice to seek one's own profit? Their advice is not only to seek profit but even to seek it at another's expense. How can the believer fellowship with the unbeliever in such a situation?

If the believer is too intimate with the unbeliever, it will be difficult not to walk after his many counsels. He will drag you away from your Christian position. If you have five unbelieving friends and they all agree in their counsel and they all think that a certain way is profitable for you, then it would be difficult for you not to follow their advice. Yet you ought not to listen to them; it only represents *their* thought.

STAND NOT IN THE WAY OF SINNERS

There are many places you should not go. Sinners have their own ways and their own places. If you are in touch with unbelievers, you will be standing with them in their way even if you do not go into the place with them. It is as if you walk your friend to the door and then depart. Though you have not entered in, you are already in the way with him. God does not want us to walk in the counsel of the wicked nor stand in the way of sinners. He desires us to keep out of the way of sinners as well as out of their place. He calls us to be wholly separated from them.

SIT NOT IN THE SEAT OF SCOFFERS

Rarely do we see unbelievers who, in the presence of a believer, do not jokingly use the name of the Lord. During the first four years of my Christian life, I met many unbelievers who so joked when I was present. They really blasphemed the name of the Lord. Can you sit among

115

these people and let the name of the Lord be blasphemed? Perhaps they never mention the Lord's name among themselves nor do they intend to blaspheme, but when you come in, their opportunity also comes. They will laugh at the Lord Jesus and ridicule Christianity. How can you sit in such a seat? In order not to sit in the seat of scoffers, you must not be intimate friends with them.

A New Kind of Friendship in the Church

Tell new believers that soon after they are saved, they need to take care of the question of friendships. They must change their friends. They should tell their former friends what has happened to them. Although they may still keep some contact, they most definitely should not continue any deep and intimate friendships. Rather, they should learn to be brothers and sisters in the church. They should substitute the brethren in the church for their former friends.

We must not be extreme. We do not hate unbelievers nor will we neglect them. But we communicate with them now on a different ground. Now we learn to witness to them and bring them to the Lord. We should only visit with them five minutes, half an hour, at most an hour. Do not sit too long and do not talk about worldly things. Learn to stand on your new position. Try your best to bring them to the Lord. Lead them to the church and preach the gospel to them. Ask some brothers or sisters to go to their homes and give the gospel to them there. Seek to make them brothers and sisters in the Lord, but do not maintain a friendship outside the realm of the brethren.

One thing I need to say: a believer who has too many

unbelieving friends is bound to fall. If he does not sin, he will at the least be worldly. It is impossible for a Christian to have many worldly friends if he loves the Lord and serves the Lord faithfully. It is wrong to have unclean lips, and it is also wrong to dwell among a people of unclean lips. It is wrong not only to sin ourselves but also to dwell among sinners. We need to confess the sin of dwelling among a people with unclean lips as well as the sin of our own unclean lips. May we ask God to give us grace that we neither sin ourselves nor desire to maintain a deep and intimate friendship with sinners.

A first question we should ask ourselves is: How good is my condition before God? A second question is: How good is my fellowship with believers? We are known to others, first, by what we are and, second, by the company we keep. If one desires to keep himself strong before God, he cannot be lax in fellowship or friendship. Once he is careless about friendships, he will immediately be defeated. New believers in particular must not be loose in this. They need to strictly separate themselves from their former friends and find those with whom they would like to fellowship in the church. Then they can have fellowship with one another in the Lord. This fellowship in the Lord should replace past communications.

Friendship in the Church

1. More Than Formal

Do you see that friends are something very special? Friendship is a relationship which transcends position. It is not formal or legal. It is a kind of fellowship which breaks through barriers of position. I have already said that some fathers and sons become friends, even though the father remains a father for life, as does the son remain a son. We also know that some mothers and daughters never become friends. Their relationship as mother and daughter is so legal that they never break beyond it. In many families, the husbands and wives are not friends; they are quite formal in their respective duties. In society, many bosses and their subordinates never become friends. Occasionally, though, it does happen. To be friends means that there is a friendship over and above the formal relationship.

ABRAHAM, GOD'S FRIEND

Sometimes man may become the friend of God. Abraham did. If Abraham had acted only formally as a man, and if God had acted only formally as God, the two could never have become friends. God had to lay aside His position, and Abraham had to forget himself in order for Abraham to become the friend of God.

CHRIST, THE SINNERS' FRIEND

The Lord Jesus is the friend of sinners. If He had stood strictly on His position, He could not have become the sinners' friend. He became a friend because He left His exalted position. Otherwise, though He could be a Savior, He could not be a friend. I hope you see what is meant by Christ being a friend. The Lord and sinners are irreconcilable. He is the Judge, and we are the judged; He is the Savior, and we are the saved. But the Lord laid all this aside to be the sinners' friend. People called Him the friend of sinners. As a friend, He is able to lead us to accept Him as our Savior.

THE APOSTLE JOHN'S FRIENDS

I believe that after a child of God has been a brother for a sufficient length of time and has come to a deeper knowledge in the Lord, he may become friends with some in the church. This naturally shows that he has transcended a formal position. This is distinctive of 3 John.

Third John was written when the apostle John was very old. Probably it was written about thirty years after Paul was martyred. When John wrote the letter, old Peter had already gone, Paul had passed away, and the rest of the twelve apostles had also departed from the world. He wrote not as an apostle but rather as an elder (v. 1). He was really advanced in age. I like his third letter. It is quite different from the other two. In 1 John he said, "Fathers," "young men," "little children," and "my little children" as if he spoke formally to them. But in the last verse of 3 John, he stood in a very special position. He would soon depart from the world. He was very old, probably in his nineties. He had known so much of the Lord and he had walked so far with God that, when writing this letter, instead of calling them brothers, sisters, little children, young men, or fathers, he said, "The friends salute thee. Salute the friends by name." Can you get the taste of it? If you can enter into the spirit of it, you will comprehend the meaning. Otherwise, you will not see. Here was a man who was so old that he outlived all his friends. Peter was dead, Paul was dead. But he could yet say, "The friends salute thee. Salute the friends by name." How very rich he was. He had arrived at the zenith of richness. For many years he had followed the Lord and had touched many things. Now he was so full of years that he could very well have patted the head of a sixty or seventy year old and called him, "My child." But he did not do this. Instead he said, "My friend." The position of formal ground was forgotten. He spoke from a position of exaltation and thus could exalt others. As the Lord became the sinners' friend, as God made Abraham His friend, so here John treats these children, young men, and fathers as friends.

2. As Brethren

Some day the young ones in the church may arrive at such an exalted place. But today they must learn to stand in the place of brethren. The matter of friendship in the church occupies a very high ground. Some day, when you are very mature, you may make little children your friends. By then you will have far exceeded them in spirituality. You will be able to exalt them to be your friends. Until that day comes, however, that which the church stresses is not friends but brothers and sisters.

Is it not something very special that the church seems to emphasize so many things except the matter of friends? It is because friendship in the church transcends position and formality and stands on a totally different ground. It is the great who exalts others to be his friends. He has become so great that he is able to lift others up by calling them friends. This, however, is not applicable to ordinary brothers and sisters. Young people and newly saved people must learn to maintain the relationship of brothers and sisters in the Lord. It is expected that they will be separated from their former friends and have fellowship with brothers and sisters in the church. This will spare them many difficulties in following the Lord.

RECREATION

All things are lawful; but not all things are expedient. All things are lawful; but not all things edify.

1 Cor. 10:23

All things are lawful for me; but not all things are expedient. All things are lawful for me; but I will not be brought under the power of any.

1 Cor. 6:12

Whether therefore ye eat, or drink, or whatsoever ye do, do all to the glory of God.

1 Cor. 10:31

The Prerequisite: Consecration

To a consecrated Christian, recreation is not a problem. Those who have trouble in this matter of recreation are those deficient in consecration. Thus, in order to solve the problem of recreation, the matter of consecration must first be resolved. Consecration is a prerequisite to the solution of the problem of recreation. What would be the use of talking about recreation if there were no consecration?

Without consecration, one would desire what God would deny.

The Purpose of Recreation

The first purpose of recreation is to meet the family's needs. It is not for ourselves that we consider this matter, but for the children in the family. To us, if we are consecrated, recreation is a very minor thing. But in our family, not only are there our own children but also there are our younger brothers and sisters. These younger ones have been entrusted to our care. If it is that they too are consecrated, the problem of recreation does not exist. However, these children, and nephews and nieces too, may not be fully consecrated; thus our attitude has much bearing upon them. What we allow or what we prohibit has a great effect upon their lives. That is why recreation is primarily a consideration for family folks, that they may give proper guidance to those of the younger generation.

The second purpose of recreation is for ourselves. A believer sometimes does need a change. The only question is how much or what kind of change is good. Adults need diversions just as the children do, but what is suitable and becoming to a Christian is something basic to settle before God. This is not too difficult for us, but for the children it may be quite necessary. What recreation will we permit our children to have? Every child of God must be clear on this. If any loopholes are left, the world will immediately invade the situation. Once in, it is not easy to drive the world away. Therefore, for the sake of keeping our family in the Lord, we must pay attention to this matter of recreation.

Principles Governing Recreation

1. NEED

Recreation according to the Lord's will grows out of a recognition of the need for it. A Christian should not go to extremes. Man does have a need for recreation. Many people are so busy that if they do not have some sort of relaxation, they may get sick and lose their health. Hence, renewal is the basic principle of recreation. This is especially important to young people. You cannot ask your children to study from morning till night. You must give them some kind of diversion, provide some change. This is a rule to be observed.

Recreation is for the sake of renewal. When one has worked five or eight hours on a project, he gets tired. When doing one thing for a long time, one's nerves get strained and one's body becomes fatigued. To refresh oneself, a change of work is needed. For example, after a child has studied for several hours at school, when he comes home he needs to play for a while. Such playing is perfectly right because it is the child's relaxation. But if the child should play eight hours in succession, his playing is more than renovation. There is a need for renewal, but to make recreation our life is unjustifiable. When a person is tired, for him to do something else for a change is right. Yet it would be wrong if he were to play from dawn to dusk. In the summer, people like to go swimming. We find no fault with it. When one is tired, it is all right to swim for half an hour or an hour. But should one immerse himself in water from morning till evening like a duck, this would no longer be recreation. We need to see the difference between recreation as renewal and recreation as our life.

When we go out to preach the gospel, sometimes we are

opposed by the saying that Christians do not have or cannot have any recreation. Those who say this do not really know what they are talking about. Actually, few people have a problem with recreation except those who overindulge in it. To be so taken up with something that you are deeply immersed in it is hardly recreation. Some people gamble three days and three nights. Their recreation has become their life. Only such people say it is difficult to be a Christian, for they have gone to extremes. What we should see, then, is that there is a need for renewal but there is no need for retrogression. There is a need for recreation but there is no need for it to become one's life. The moment one lives in it, he falls into error. "All things are lawful for me; but not all things are expedient. All things are lawful for me; but I will not be brought under the power of any." It is a great error to be controlled by anything.

2. Possible Forms

Recreation may take many different forms. A Christian might enjoy any of the following:

REST

The best form of recreation for a Christian is rest. I am tired today, so I rest a while. The Lord Jesus and His disciples were tired working, so He told them, "Come ye yourselves apart into a desert place, and rest a while" (Mark 6:31). His rest includes the idea of recreation. He does not say, "Rest a while," but He says, "Come . . . apart into a desert place and rest a while." Oftentimes our fatigue is relieved after resting beside the hill or the water. The most common form of Christian recreation is rest.

CHANGE OF WORK

Sometimes you can feel yourself becoming dull and inactive. If so, take a change by working on something else. Usually you work eight hours. Take out two hours to do some other work. If you always work sitting, stand up for a change. If your work is mental work, change to a little physical exertion and immediately your weariness will be gone. Though this is not what the world calls recreation, yet, by changing your work, you may get rid of your tiredness. Furthermore, this is something you can easily arrange to do. Since the principle of recreation is renewal, a change of work fits the requirement.

HOBBIES

There are many hobbies proper for a Christian. Some people like to take pictures. Some like to keep a bird or two. Some like to plant flowers. Some like to paint. All these are legitimate and within a proper Christian domain. Some may like music, such as playing the piano or writing musical compositions. Others may like to practice calligraphy. Any of these is appropriate.

However, there is a principle governing any recreation: you must be able to lay it down as well as take it up. If you cannot lay it down, something is wrong. For example, it is innocent to take pictures and research a bit into photography. But do not let it influence you too much. If you are well along on the spiritual course, these things will not disturb you. But it would be wrong for you to feel you *must* take pictures. You should be able both to take it up and to lay it down. A young Christian may play the violin a little, but it is wrong if he cannot lay it down. The difficulty with the new Christian is that he finds it very hard to lay down his particular recreation. If that is the case, he may have to sell his violin. Otherwise he cannot be a good Christian, for he is held by his violin. Christian recreation is to be able to play the violin or to lay it down. It is to not be under the power of the violin. This is a principle that needs to be remembered.

Another illustration: Suppose some young brothers like to collect stamps. There is nothing wrong with it; on the contrary, it may be quite helpful. Through stamp collecting they learn something of the geography and history of the nations of the world. But they must not be enslaved by it. That which helps to refresh a person but does not possess him is considered a legitimate recreation.

Parents should lead their children into proper recreation. If they do not, the children will seek improper pastimes. I have seen some children who were damaged by their ultra-strict parents. Their homes were more like factories. The result was that these children slipped outside to engage in improper recreation. Parents must clearly understand that children need some recreation. If it is not provided, they will look upon their homes as dry and tasteless. They may even steal away from school in order to play.

GAMES

There are many games of skill such as chess, ball games, and riding which are commendable. Although there is the element of victory and defeat, they are nonetheless proper because they are entirely games of skill. It is well to let the children play table tennis or basketball or tennis or chess. There is nothing inherently sinful in these games. Parents should be more lenient with their children in such things. Older people may not have time for strenuous sports, but they should not hinder the young from engaging in such games. True, we want them to spend their time for the Lord, but they do also need some recreation. Let us be glad to let them have it.

Thus far we have mentioned four kinds of recreation—rest, a change of work, a hobby, and games. All these are permissible for Christians. But a Christian must never be under the power of any of them. To be under their control is an error.

3. To Help Us Work

Why do we need recreation? It is to help us work better. Recreation has a purpose; it is not an end it itself. I do not play ball just because I like to play ball. I play ball that I may work better. I do not sleep just because I love to sleep. I sleep so that I may work better. I do not plant flowers just for enjoyment but so that I may work efficiently. These things are permissible only because they help us work better and serve God in a stronger way. They should never be a disturbance to us. Sometimes you see people work on one thing day and night. If they continue like this for two or three weeks, their mind and their physical strength will be exhausted. It would be better for them to seek the Lord about having some diversion. After working seven or eight hours, they should change their work—play the piano or play ball. Such diversion is for the purpose of restoration. It is to increase, not decrease, their efficiency. Because of the refreshment of recreation, their work can be better done and thus they can serve God in a stronger way.

Sometimes it may be good for you to travel a bit. The Lord Jesus did that when He went to the desert for a rest. Or you may play ball with your children at home. Do not view this as an entanglement, but as something that helps your work. Should it make your work worse, then it is not on the right principle. Recreation must be a help to your work. When the day's work is over, you may benefit from jogging a while or doing some gardening. It is not that we desire to promote these things, but we do want to permit them.

To have a two or three month vacation is all right. To have a two or three day holiday after a month's labor is permissible. But to have a holiday every day is simply laziness. Christians must know how to work; they must not be lazy. We suggest recreation only to increase our working efficiency, but our recreation must not be such as to bring criticism. Let us not overdo in anything so that the name of God may be glorified in us.

4. NO GAMES OF CHANCE

There is a special requirement as to what games should be allowed: all games must involve skill. None of them should be pure chance. A game is commendable only if it depends on skill, not on chance. If it requires both skill and chance, it becomes a gamble. If it is all chance and no skill, it most definitely is gambling. Games which Christians play must be games of skill, not of chance. Dice is purely a game of chance. It is gambling and Christians should not be involved in it. The young may play chess and checkers because it is a matter of skill, not of chance.

All games may be divided into two kinds: skill or chance. Christians should not be engaged in any kind of gambling, for gambling is based on chance. Some people before they were saved played Mah-Jongg (a Chinese gambling game). Such a game is gambling because it needs chance as well as skill. Even if money is not involved, games of that type still stir in people the hope that they may be helped by luck.

By their very nature some things are gambling, while other things, though not essentially gambling, can be used that way. To play dice is gambling whether or not money is involved. Its nature is gambling and therefore Christians ought not engage in it. The principle which decides is: If it is a game of chance, it is wrong, for anything that is accomplished by chance is a gamble. Skill is something that belongs to you, but chance is beyond you. Whatever people generally think of as gambling, we Christians should not touch, for we live by principle.

5. SUITED TO THE NEED

Our recreation must meet our need. Because we have a need, we therefore have such and such a recreation. If there is no need, then there is no recreation required. Some brothers in the church, though quite busy, have no need for recreation. Others may do nothing all day but yet feel a need. Those who feel the greatest need for renewal may need it the least, while those who sense the least need may actually need it most. Hence, let us not talk much about renewal. Instead of telling God's people in a general way that it is all right to have recreation, let us tell them to judge for themselves if they really have such a need. The rule that governs everything is that my time is all His; therefore, how can I best live for the Lord?

Life is measured by time. Of course, life is more than just time, but it is measured by it. To spend an hour is to spend an hour of your life. If you spend an hour in recreation, this hour must in return help your work. Without such a need, to spend the hour is to waste time, and a waste of time is a waste of life. That hour could have been given to the Lord with more results. If I spend it in recreation, it is an investment from which I expect to be able to work better. If I can work better afterward, then there is no waste involved. Remember, if there is need, it is not a waste. If there is not a need, it is a waste.

Sometimes those older in the Lord may tell you that you need some relaxation because you are too tense. Sometimes the doctor may warn you not to continue at such a pace lest you impair your health. Such recreation is for the sake of need, not for the sake of play. It is not an end in itself but to enable you to work better. A busy person may or may not need recreation, depending on his need.

Those young in age do need recreation. Parents should not deprive the children of meeting the need for recreation just because they themselves have no such need. To deprive the children is to push them toward sinful recreation.

6. HEALTHY FOR THE BODY

All recreation must be agreeable to the body. This is one of the first principles: the recreation must benefit the body. So, before entering into recreation, one should consider whether or not it is of physical benefit. If the recreation should damage the body, it is in violation of a first principle and is highly questionable. For example, if a brother has tuberculosis, his recreation must be of a nature not to adversely affect his sickness. Or if a sister has heart trouble, she may need some *light* recreation to help relieve her fatigue yet not affect her heart.

I hope we may see that our whole body belongs to the Lord. If we refresh ourselves, it is for the Lord, and if we do not, it is also for the Lord. Nothing is for ourselves.

When we have recreation, let us do it for the Lord's sake. When we do not have it, let it also be for His sake. Whether we have or have not, the principle is to not hurt the body. If the presence or absence of recreation hurts our body it is a loss. Not only is it wrong for us to destroy our body with improper things; also it is wrong to destroy our body with proper tasks. The body of a child of God does not belong to him. Hence, in considering recreation, always consider whether or not it would be good for the body. If good, do it; if not, refrain from it. The question should not be decided on the basis of likes or dislikes. If a sister with heart trouble is attracted by the ball game the brothers outside are playing, and joins in with them, she may suffer the consequences of it. It is not wrong for the brothers to play, but for that sister to play is wrong. May all the children of God see that everything we do is for serving God. If we engage in some recreation, our purpose is to serve God better.

I do not expect believers to die in their youth. My hope is that there will be elderly brothers and sisters in the church. There is a great difference between the elderly in the world and the elderly in the church. In the world, the more elderly one is, the more apt he is to be set and backward, whereas the younger are more apt to be forward-looking. But in the church, it is the advanced in age who are more forward-looking. In the world, if the aged do not die, many new things will be pushed down and progress held up. But in the church, it is quite different. The older ones are the newer, for they touch deeper and higher in spiritual things. If a church should lack elderly brothers and sisters, it will be poor and weak. So I do not anticipate brothers and sisters in the church dying early because of neglect of their bodies. Such a death would deprive the church of the supply of Christ from the lessons he has learned in the Lord. Before he has been able to supply the church, he has already died. The church should not have such a loss; it cannot bear such loss.

We should not engage in sports for the sake of competition or recordbreaking as many athletes do. We play only to benefit our bodies.

7. PLEASURABLE TO THE INDIVIDUAL

What recreation we choose is related not only to our body but also to our disposition. If you do what you like to do, it tends to restore your brain power, ease your nerve, and relax your emotions. That which you do not like is more like work than recreation. Here is a sister who loves flowers. You give her half an hour to water the flowers. Instead of being tired by it, she feels refreshed after that half hour of watering. Her tense nerves and emotions are relaxed. But if you ask another person who dislikes flowers to water them for half an hour, to that person it becomes a burden. Hence, recreation is related to disposition. In choosing recreation, one must choose that which helps to loosen his nerves and relieve his tensions. Everyone has his own type of recreation. To some, watering flowers is recreation; to others, it is not. Some love puppies and kittens; others are afraid of them and find no recreation in playing with them. Some relax with things that cause tenseness in others. Therefore, let each one find the recreation which pleases him and which helps him work.

8. NOT A STUMBLING BLOCK

As Christians, we must be examples in all things. Even in the matter of recreation, we must not be a stumbling block to others. We live for our brethren as well as for the Lord; we do not live for ourselves. As Christians we are highly influential. We must therefore be concerned not only for ourselves, but also for others. God asks Christians to be as contagious as the plague. We cannot murmur and say, "Why do people look to us?" Whom else can they look to if not to us? Of course they will look at us. Who can fail to see the city that is built on the hill? Who will not see the light on the mountain? No matter how we ourselves feel, we must consider how the younger brothers and sisters will be affected by us. Will we stumble them in the things that we do? We are God's children; we have believed in the Lord. Hereafter we must cultivate a delicate sensitivity. We are responsible not only to God but also to our many brothers and sisters.

I myself sense that I may eat meat. It is not a problem to me. But if my eating meat will stumble others, I will not eat it. Not that my eating meat is wrong, but my stumbling others is. Likewise, there may be nothing wrong with my recreation, but it is wrong for me to stumble my brothers.

In the things that we do, we must consider what the weak will think. We do not want to be a stumbling block to those feeble in faith. The word of the Lord is: "Take heed lest by any means this liberty of yours become a stumblingblock to the weak" (1 Cor. 8:9). Though we know an idol is nothing, yet we do not go to idol temples for the sake of the weak consciences of some Christians. To them an idol *is* something. Let this principle of not being a stumbling block govern all our actions. That which might stumble others, let us not do.

What should you do if your conscience is peaceful about something but someone else's is not? You cannot just consider your own peace if someone else is disturbed. For his sake, refrain from doing it. If it might be that someone else would be stumbled, do not argue that you personally would not be. True, you might not sin, but consider that, through you, he might be led into sin because of this very matter. For the sake of other brothers and sisters, then, there are many kinds of recreation which we cannot do. All things are lawful to us, but not all are expedient. When we talk to young brothers and sisters, we must help them to see that they must walk circumspectly before God. Have some recreation, but refrain from that which may stumble others. Be especially careful of those who might easily be offended or entangled.

9. Not Considered Improper

Whatever recreation unbelievers judge improper, we Christians should not take up. Even certain kinds of recreation which they do approve, we still may not take up. These are the two rules about recreation in relation to unbelievers. What they disapprove, we certainly do not allow. And even what they approve we may not accept. To frequent theatres, to dance, to gamble—we do not approve.

It is not worthwhile to argue with people about recreation. For example: suppose in a certain place, it is commonly thought that playing ball is not permissible. Since our testimony is for the Lord and not for the ball, we just keep quiet. There is no need for us to sermonize on the justification of playing ball. Also remember that our standard cannot be lower than that of the unbelievers. If the Gentiles in a certain locality consider chess taboo, let us not speak for it. Let us not waste even an hour advocating the correctness of chess playing. Our desire is to witness for the Lord, not to try to encourage these minor things. Indeed, let us not even do them. Whatever thing the people of a locality judge as wrong, be it even such an innocent thing as fishing, let us refrain from doing it. Our standard cannot be lower than that of the unbelievers. This is especially applicable to recreation.

It is very foolish to argue with people over the question of recreation. Some missionaries have had a very bad relationship with the natives of a place because of insisting on a particular recreation. I think it is wrong to damage one's work for the sake of a little recreation. Let us concentrate on the essentials and leave the non-essentials. If some brothers are led to go to a Moslem area, can they openly eat pork because Christians are allowed to? Eating pork is tabooed in that area, so, for the sake of the work, do not create trouble by these minor things. If you should go to Sikon [adjacent to Tibet] where people never go fishing, then you too should not fish. Otherwise it would not be right.

All these nine principles should be laid before the new believers. Lead them to deal carefully with the matter of recreation in the light of these principles.

Recreation Does Not Affect Spirituality

Lastly, let me relate to you a simple story: the Keswick Convention is a big gathering in England. It may be regarded as a very special conference. Every year people from all over the world gather there for a week. The attendance usually numbers five or six thousand. I believe this convention has been especially blessed of God. Among those who have spoken there was Evan Hopkins, who was called the theologian of Keswick. He was among the first to see the truth of our co-death with Christ. Hopkins was really a fine person before the Lord. Also, he had a hobby. Whenever he was free, he liked to draw pictures. At first, he drew rather conventionally. After he had granddaughters, though, he drew only rabbits. Whenever he came back from preaching, he would draw these rabbits for his granddaughters. Before his life was over, he had drawn several thousand rabbits! Later on, some publishers put out a book of Hopkins' rabbits. As you look at these drawings, you can see that Hopkins was a clever person. The face of every rabbit is different. Another hobby Hopkins had was writing small prints. He did the whole of the Lord's prayer on a shilling piece. I mention this, not with the intention of urging you to imitate him, but to impress upon you that recreation does not hinder a person's spirituality. To the contrary, it often reveals the inner character of that person. God's servants are not all of a dull type by any means! That would not be Christian. To be Christian is to be innocent, simple, and natural.

Another person you may remember was George Muller. He was one who knew how to pray. When a girl by the name of Abigail asked him to pray for a colored woolen ball, he did pray for her and she did get the ball. Later she became a well known person in England. If you read her biography, you will see how deeply she was taught in the Lord. If the recreation is appropriate, it will not drag you down. By keeping these basic principles, recreation can uplift you and restore your mind and body to functioning properly.

SPEECH

Speech Comes Out of the Heart

"For out of the abundance of the heart the mouth speaketh" (Matt. 12:34), the Lord Jesus said. Man's speech represents his heart; it reveals what is there. One's actions do not always declare the person, but his word often does. Actions may be so careful as to mislead people, but speech is not so easily guarded as to be under perfect control. Thus speech reveals more clearly what is in the mind of a person. Out of the abundance of the heart, out of what is stored within, the mouth speaks. If a lie or deception is expressed by the mouth, it must be also in the heart. When a person is silent, it is difficult to know his heart. But once he opens his mouth, his heart is unveiled. Before he speaks, no one can fathom his spirit. When he speaks, though, others may touch his spirit and discern his condition before God.

Having trusted in the Lord, we must learn afresh how to live and how to speak. Old things and old ways are passed away. Today we start anew.

How to Speak

There are a few passages in the Bible which teach us how to speak. Let us look at them one by one.

1. WITHOUT LIES

"You are of your father the devil, and the lusts of your father it is your will to do. He was a murderer from the beginning, and standeth not in the truth, because there is no truth in him. When he speaketh a lie, he speaketh of his own: for he is a liar, and the father thereof" (John 8:44).

SATAN THE FATHER OF LIARS

When Satan speaks a lie, he speaks from himself, for he is a liar. But today he is more than a liar; he is the father of all liars. How prevalent lies are in this world. There are as many liars as there are subjects of Satan. They lie for him because he needs the lie to establish his kingdom and to upset God's work. Everyone who belongs to Satan knows how to lie and how to do a lying work.

As soon as one is saved, he must learn the basic lesson of dealing with his words. He must learn to resist all lies, whether spoken knowingly or unknowingly, and he must refrain from uttering inaccurate words, words that are either less or more than the truth. Lies of all kinds must be removed from the midst of God's children. If any trace remains, Satan has some ground to attack.

LIES MOST PREVALENT

Until one learns to resist lying, he may not be conscious of how prone he is to lie. But the more he refuses to lie, the more he discovers how easy it is for him to do so. Even the thoughts and intents of his heart incline toward lying. The lies in the world, nay even the lies in us, are far beyond our imagination. How pitiful it is that, to many of God's children, an "occasional" lie seems indispensable. How tragic that any lie has a place among the children of God. Does not our Lord's word make it sufficiently clear and serious that all who lie are the children of Satan, for he is the father of all liars? It would be a sad thing if this seed of Satan should still remain ingrained in the heart of God's own. So, to new believers we say, do not allow much time to pass before you determine to deal strictly with the problem of lying.

MEANING OF LIES

The double-tongued person is a liar. He will say one thing one time and another thing another time. He says "yes" now and "no" later, "right" now and "wrong" later. This not only shows a weakness of mind but also shows that he is a liar.

Lying also means speaking according to our personal preference. If we say only what we like to say and hide the rest, or if we utter only what serves us and leave off that which does not serve us, we are telling lies. How often we purposely keep back half of a matter. Our selfishness prompts us to hold back that part which is profitable. To those whom we dislike, we tell that which is unprofitable, even harmful to them. This too is lying. Many people do not speak according to what is true but according to their likes and dislikes. They speak what their emotion dictates rather than the pure facts. They adjust their words in accordance with whom or what they like or dislike. Such words are based on personal preference or emotion, not on fact or truth. They should be classified as lies. To speak untruthfully is sinful, but to wilfully speak an untruth is even more sinful. God utterly condemns that. Young believers need to be shown that they must not speak according to their emotion but according to fact. Either keep silent or speak the truth.

To speak according to what one hopes is lying. We must learn to discipline our emotion to such an extent that our speech is not governed by our interest or expectation. Many times the words uttered do not stand for facts; they represent, rather, what is hoped for. People speak evilly of others not because these evils are factual, but because the one speaking hopes it is that way. He longs that his brothers or sisters in the Lord may fall; then he can gloatingly say that they have fallen. Thus his words express what he wishes as if it were a fact, not what the fact really is. Do you see the basic difficulty here? People often speak according to the wishes of their hearts, according to what they are hoping for.

Injecting one's own thought is lying. Why is it that a word is completely altered after it passes several times from person to person? It is because each person adds his own thought to it. Instead of seeking to know the facts, each one injects his own idea. This must also be considered as lying. Young believers need to learn from the beginning how to speak according to the facts. They should not mingle in their own opinions. At the least, they should indicate what is fact and what is opinion. It is quite evident that what you think of a person and what he really is are two separate things. At the most, you may say the fact is such and such, but this is how I think. Beware lest you overly stress your thought and expectation so that the facts are changed and it degenerates into a lie.

Another lie which is quite prevalent in the church is exaggerated speech. How easy it is to give an inaccurate number and to use an inexact word. How tempting to employ big, strong words to magnify beyond the truth. This, too, is a lie; it is not according to the fact.

You may test the heart condition of a brother or a sister by telling him or her something and asking that it be passed on. Almost immediately you will find out his heart condition before God. One who fears God and who has been dealt with by God will not dare speak carelessly; he knows the seriousness of speech and he will try his best to pass the word on accurately. But he who is undisciplined will add many of his own words to it and he also will hold back much which ought to be said. He is a careless, dishonest person.

No one who lies is fit to be a minister of God's Word. Only one accurate in speech can understand the Bible, for every jot and tittle of the Word of God is most exact. If we are careless, who knows how many jots and tittles we miss?

Inflating a number is a lie. Many are so used to doing this that they invariably enlarge any amount they touch upon. For example, we know that no church building in Shanghai can accommodate as many as five thousand people. But at revival meetings people will say that they have ten or twenty thousand in their church. Even if the occupants were to stand, that would still be too many for any church building in Shanghai. Yet such boastings come from Christians, nay, from Christian workers! This kind of boasting is without doubt a lie.

Also, we tend to enlarge others' faults and minimize our own. This too is a lie.

STRICT DISCIPLINE NEEDED

I cannot say that after people are saved they necessarily have become honest people. But if they will learn under

God's strict discipline, we may, after five years, meet some who have become honest. Perhaps my words sound harsh but I do emphasize them. Unless one resists every lie and every inaccurate word relentlessly for years, he is not an honest person. No one who neglects such discipline should even expect to be honest. It is an all too common illness among Christians to tell lies and to speak inaccurately. People in the world (we were once such), having followed Satan, all know how to lie. The wise among them as well as the foolish know how to lie. Some speak bluntly, others speak skillfully; yet all speak lies. We need to be so disciplined before God that we may be sensitive to lies and to a lying spirit as soon as we meet it.

New believers need to see how important honesty is and yet how unnatural it is to us. Our very nature is dishonest; we have known how to lie from childhood. We like to speak according to our preferences rather than according to truth. So, even as a child must learn his ABC's, so must God's children start from the very beginning. Otherwise a slight carelessness will plunge us once again into telling a lie or speaking inaccurately.

Many people regard telling a lie as a light matter, but I personally judge it as one of the darkest and most common sins. If a new believer has this ailment in his speech, two difficulties will result: (1) Much spiritual death will be produced in the church, making it impossible for the Christians to be one, and (2) God will be unable to choose such a person to be a minister of His Word. Though that one may try to lecture on the Bible, teach the truth, or preach the Word, yet he is disqualified from being a true minister of God's Word. To be a minister of God's Word requires that a person be honest in his speaking.

Therefore learn to speak as before God. Speak accurately. Avoid all lies. Do not speak according to your own preference or opinion. Resist all lies absolutely. Speaking should be objective, not subjective, in nature. It should be according to fact or truth.

2. WITHOUT IDLE WORDS

"The good man out of his good treasure bringeth forth good things: and the evil man out of his evil treasure bringeth forth evil things. And I say unto you, that every idle word that men shall speak, they shall give account thereof in the day of judgment. For by thy words thou shalt be justified, and by thy words thou shalt be condemned" (Matt. 12:35-37 .

Verses 35-37 should be connected with verse 33 which says: "Either make the tree good, and its fruit good; or make the tree corrupt, and its fruit corrupt: for the tree is known by its fruit." We can readily see that the fruit here refers to words rather than to conduct. If a man is good, his words assuredly will be good; if he is evil, then his words no doubt will be evil also. By listening to his words, you may know what sort of person he is. Should he sow seeds of contention from morning to night, criticizing people, speaking slanderously and destructively, and using dirty words, he is definitely a corrupt tree.

It will not help for a brother or a sister who continually speaks evil, critical, sinful words to try to correct his or her statements. Rather, he or she should be bluntly told that to gossip at all is profane. New believers need to know that their words are their fruits. One whose heart is holy will speak purely. One whose heart is full of love will not utter words of hate. By its fruit the tree is known.

Not every fact should be told. Though some words may be true, if they are not the kind of fruit I want to bear, I should not repeat them. The question now is not whether the words are a fact, but whether I should say them. It is a question of idle words. Though the words are true, they may be idly spoken. Whatever we say must be according to fact, but not all facts should be spoken. If the facts constitute idle words, they should not be uttered.

Idle words spoken once will again be spoken: "And I say unto you, that every idle word that men shall speak, they shall give account thereof in the day of judgment." Whatever is inadvertently said today will be repeated verbatim in the future on the day of judgment. Every word will then be taken into account; by these words a person shall either be justified or condemned. May God's children learn to fear God by resisting all incorrect words and by speaking accurately. Whatever is unprofitable for others and for me or is unrelated to me should not be said.

No disciplined person can have a loose tongue. It is by a person's tongue that discipline or lack of it can be seen. A person disciplined by God also has a disciplined tongue. He who lies, tells idle words, or speaks carelessly is not of much use in the hand of God. He waits for the judgment to come. Therefore, new believers ought to learn this lesson. He who uses unclean words must himself be unclean; he who speaks dishonestly must be a dishonest person. The kind of speech reveals the kind of person. By its fruit the tree is known; by his speech the person is revealed.

Alas, the church today has fallen to such a degree that she is filled with lies and idle words. Very few of God's children are really conscious of this sin and dare to condemn it. This is appalling.

3. WITHOUT EVIL WORDS

"Not rendering evil for evil, or reviling for reviling; but contrariwise blessing; for hereunto were ye called, that ye should inherit a blessing. For, he that would love life, and see good days, let him refrain his tongue from evil, and his lips that they speak no guile: And let him turn away from evil, and do good; let him seek peace, and pursue it. For the eyes of the Lord are upon the righteous, and his ears unto their supplication: but the face of the Lord is upon them that do evil" (1 Pet. 3:9–12).

One kind of word which should never come from a Christian's mouth is evil words. Evil words are words of reviling, words of cursing. A child of God cannot return evil for evil, or insult for insult.

SAY WORDS OF BLESSING

Men like to argue. When others speak evilly, Christians sometimes use the same words. But the Lord does not ask who spoke first, He just questions whether you said that. Remember, you cannot render evil for evil, reviling for reviling. So, learn instead to say words of blessing.

CONTROL YOUR TEMPER

Only the man who controls his temper is able to control his word before God. If his temper is not controlled, many evil words, nay, even low, base, insulting words will come from his mouth. This will not only deprive him of blessing before God but will also bring disgrace upon God.

4. WITHOUT MANY WORDS

In the Bible, James 3 deals especially with the matter of speech. We will choose a few of these verses for consideration.

NOT MANY TEACHERS

"Be not many of you teachers, my brethren" (v. 1). It may be translated either, "Be not teachers of many," or

"Be not teachers." Why does Scripture say this? "Knowing that we shall receive heavier judgment." Those who do not know how to control their words are easily manifested by their eagerness to be teachers. Wherever they go, they teach. Wherever they are, they talk. They are able to teach others under any circumstance. They teach freely, without cost. They like to be teachers; they itch to be counselors. Whenever they are around, they are talkative. Do you see that a Christian should not only refrain from telling a lie or speaking idly or evilly, but should also restrain himself from much speaking? No matter what he says, too much of it is never right. It robs him of God's blessing.

THE MARK OF SELF-CONTROL

"For in many things we all stumble. If any stumbleth not in word, the same is a perfect man, able to bridle the whole body also" (v. 2). Whether or not one can bridle himself hinges on whether he is able to bridle his words. To judge if he has the fruit of the Spirit in self-control, one only needs to observe how he controls his words. Do you know what self-control is? Oftentimes brothers and sisters have a wrong concept about the matter. They think that self-control as the fruit of the Holy Spirit means moderation, the middle way. No, self-control here means nothing but control over self, bridling oneself.

In other words, to be able to control oneself is the fruit of the Holy Spirit. What is the mark of this fruit of the Holy Spirit by which it can be recognized? James tells us that if a man is able to bridle his tongue he can bridle his whole body. Such a man has self-control. A loose tongue betrays a loose life. He who speaks thoughtlessly leads a careless

146

life. Too much speaking dissipates a person. May young believers start to learn to bridle their words.

Do you wish that God in His mercy would deal with you? Let me tell you: if He is able to deal with your words, then He has found *the* way to deal with you. For many people, their words are the center of their being. Their words serve as their backbone. Discipline the words and the person is disciplined. If the matter of one's words resists breaking, the person remains unchanged. In order to determine whether one can control himself, do not look at his outward appearance (for that may be deceiving); just talk with him for half an hour or so. Then you will know. As soon as one talks, he is known. Nothing reveals a person more than his words.

THE GREAT INFLUENCE OF THE TONGUE

James 3, verse 3 compares the tongue to a horse's bridle, verse 4 to a ship's rudder, and verse 5 to a small fire. Small as a bridle or a rudder or a spark, the tongue nevertheless can assert great influence. Verse 6 further says, "And the tongue is a fire: the world of iniquity among our members is the tongue, which defileth the whole body, and setteth on fire the wheel of nature, and is set on fire by hell." Indeed, the tongue is a world of iniquity, a world of its own. If the tongue of a Christian has not been especially dealt with, it will yet kindle hell fire and spread death everywhere.

How serious this is: "setteth on fire the wheel of nature." Life is like a wheel which turns; the tongue is like a fire which kindles the wheel. Many works of the flesh are thus exploded. Man's temper, his wrath, his flesh are all set on fire by the tongue, and it is a hell fire. How many times things flare up because of some words spoken by a child of God. The tongue is truly a world of iniquity and a fire from hell.

Therefore, let us learn to speak less. "In the multitude of words there wanteth not transgression; but he that refraineth his lips doeth wisely" (Prov. 10:19). The book of Proverbs persuades us to refrain from much speaking. Only fools are profuse in words. The more foolish a person is, the more he talks. Disciplined persons, however, are firm and few in words.

THE EVIL OF THE TONGUE

Verse 7 tells us that every kind of living creature has been tamed by mankind. Verse 8 continues with "the tongue can no man tame; it is a restless evil, it is full of deadly poison." Some evils can be tamed, but the evil of the tongue no man can tame. How foolish it is to set the tongue loose.

TWO KINDS OF WATER

What follows is quite simple. You must not use the same tongue on the one hand to praise God and on the other hand to curse men made after the likeness of God. How can you on one side praise and on the other side curse? A fountain cannot send forth two kinds of water; a fig tree cannot yield both olives and figs; neither can salt water yield sweet. The kind of fruit shows the type of tree; the nature of the water reveals the source of the fountain. A person used of God is he who yields only sweet water, in whom there is neither curse nor bitterness.

God has so delivered me that He has put a new fountain in me. He has made me a new tree. If I be a fig tree, I cannot yield olives. If I be a vine, I will not yield figs. Since

God has put a new life within me, I naturally send forth sweet water.

How to Listen

In considering the matter of speech, we must pay attention to listening as well as to speaking.

1. RESIST AN ITCHING EAR

May I be frank with you? If brothers and sisters knew how to listen, the church would be rid of many improper words. The reason there are so many inappropriate words in the church is because so many want to hear them. Since there is such a desire, there is such a source of supply. Why should men have so much destructive criticism, wicked slandering, double-talk, unclean words, lies, and words of contention? It is because so many are willing to listen. How treacherous and crooked and defiled is the human heart that itches to hear such unedifying words.

If God's children knew what kind of words to speak and what kind not to, they would quite naturally know what to listen to and what not to listen to. What you listen to betrays you; it reveals what kind of person you are.

New believers ought to learn to listen properly. If anyone sows seeds of strife and uses improper words, not only should you resist the temptation to do so yourself but also you should refuse to hear him. By so doing, you will put an end to many sins and at the same time help other brothers and sisters to resist too. There is today a hearing lust, a lust to hear unsuitable words. No wonder the number of such improper words increases; no wonder those who say them feel encouraged to do so. Let us learn to walk away quietly and leave people alone when they talk such nonsense. Then they will soon lose interest in such wanton talk. Or, instead of walking away, we may testify and say that as Christians we should not say these things. Or we may even remonstrate with them, saying, "What kind of person do you think I am? I do not want to hear such rubbish."

Many difficulties in the church are like hell fire which must be quenched as soon as it is started. Such difficulties should not be allowed to spread. Many of them may be caused by hearing amiss. Although the speaker must bear the greater part of the responsibility, the hearer has his lesser share too. In order to be delivered from the lust of knowing things, man needs to resist the natural inclination to want to hear words. If he is able to resist this lust, he can quench many fires. Learn to say, "I am sorry, I cannot listen to such words because I am a Christian." Learn to cut short such words. But if you listen, hoping to learn more, you are not quenching the fire but stirring it up.

2. TURN A DEAF EAR

"But I, as a deaf man, hear not; and I am as a dumb man that openeth not his mouth. Yea, I am as a man that heareth not, and in whose mouth are no reproofs" (Ps. 38:13–14). When people talk improperly, be as a deaf man who does not hear. Let them say what they like, but do not listen. Or, instead of being as one deaf, you may testify to them, even reprove them, by saying, "Who do you think I am that you pour all that rubbish on me? I think a Christian should not say these things. They are not suitable for a believer." There is great blessing in learning to be deaf and dumb, for talking and listening are tremendous temptations. May young believers know how to overcome.

150

3. EXAMPLE OF THE LORD

"Who is blind, but my servant? or deaf, as my messenger that I send? who is blind as he that is at peace with me, and blind as Jehovah's servant?" (Is. 42:19). This verse, in the context of the chapter, refers to the Lord Jesus. "Who is deaf as my messenger" shows how the Lord Jesus on earth turned a deaf ear to many words.

Hearing less of these unclean words and unrelated things means having less trouble. We have enough problems of our own without unnecessarily adding more. How can we run our course if we are overloaded? Learn, therefore, to resist the temptation to hear. Be as deaf as the Lord Jesus. The man who is as deaf as our Lord has a straight way.

Spend Time to Learn

Young believers need to be wise as to speech, both in speaking and in hearing. Let them fear God in what they say and hear. This is a big thing; it must be learned attentively and patiently.

It takes time to develop the habit of speaking accurately. I do not think we can attain victory in this area very soon after we believe in the Lord. I know from experience that it is rather hard to speak accurately. A little carelessness and a word may be wrongly said; even the intention may be wrong.

"Set a watch, O Jehovah, before my mouth; keep the doors of my lips" (Ps. 141:3). How we need this prayer: set a watch before my mouth that I may not speak carelessly. Perhaps some should pray, "Set a watch over my ears that I may not hear indiscriminately"! If such prayers are offered, the church will be saved many troubles; new believers will be able to walk in the right course.

One thing surprises me greatly: many brothers and sisters listen without feeling uncomfortable. Evidently something is drastically wrong. Whenever we are able to lend our ears to improper speech, something is wrong with us. If we listen and accept it, we are greatly wrong. Therefore, we must learn to resist such defiled and corrupt fruit. We should know that if there is any poison among God's children it will inevitably spread. It will lead people into ungodliness and rebellion.

May God be gracious and merciful to us. May He give grace to all new believers that they may start at once to learn how to speak and how to hear so that there may be a straight path before them. It is not unusual to hear God's children speaking heedlessly, but it is strange that a Christian can speak or hear such heedless words without being conscious that they are sinful and without condemning them. May such a thing not happen among the new believers.

CLOTHING AND EATING

We have before us the practical matter of a Christian's clothing and food.

Clothing

1. ITS MEANING

In order to find the meaning of clothing, we must trace it back to the beginning.

BEFORE THE FALL

Before the fall, probably Adam and Eve were clothed with light. They were innocent. Although they both were naked, they were not ashamed.

AFTER THE FALL

After sin came in, the first effect was the opening of Adam and Eve's eyes to their nakedness. Immediately they felt ashamed and sewed fig leaves to make themselves aprons. So the basic meaning of clothing is for covering. Clothes are used to cover nakedness. The aprons made of fig leaves could not have lasted long, for the leaves would soon dry and break into pieces. God therefore clothed Adam and Eve with the more enduring coats of skin. His purpose was to cover the body.

We should tell new believers that the meaning of clothing is for covering, not for exposure! Any dress which is not for covering is questionable; any purpose other than to cover is also wrong. *Clothing is for covering.*

THE NEED FOR BLOOD

In the land of Judea, the Hebrews wore sandals without socks. Hence, only the feet, hands, and head were exposed. The rest of the body was all covered by clothing. Those who study the Bible will recall how, at the time of cleansing, the blood was applied on the thumb of the right hand, the big toe of the right foot, and the tip of the right ear (see Lev. 14). These three exposed areas were covered by the blood. Blood was not applied to other parts of the body because they were covered by clothing. So the purpose of clothing is to cover. It is appropriate to be properly clothed before God.

Today's failure lies in the tendency to drift more and more toward barbarism, to be scantily clothed. Clothing which is not for covering violates God's thought. The spiritual significance of the blood is to deny exposure. Once man sinned, he needed to be covered before God. This covering is an absolute necessity. Any shortening of sleeves and hems to expose the body instead of to cover it is worldly.

Therefore, according to the meaning of clothing, it is better to be adequately covered. Being a sinner, I wish to be completely covered in the sight of God. I do not want any area to be uncovered. As a Christian, I have no ground on which to stand before God unless the Lord wholly covers me. I ask the Lord to so cover me that my whole being is redeemed, that what the clothes leave uncovered the blood covers. My hands, my feet, and my head are all under the blood.

THE SECOND FALL

When Adam and Eve sinned, their nakedness was seen. One thousand six hundred fifty-six years later, Noah stepped out of the ark. He planted a vineyard, and he became drunk. As a result he took off his clothes and uncovered himself. Adam, the first man, found he was naked after he ate the fruit of the tree of the knowledge of good and evil; Noah uncovered himself after drinking the wine made of grapes. The fall of Adam was from no need of clothing to the need for clothing; the fall of Noah was from being covered to being uncovered.

PLACEMENT OF THE ALTAR

After the exodus of the people of Israel from Egypt, God gave the law at Mount Sinai. He commanded the Israelites to build an altar low enough to not need steps. Why? "Neither shalt thou go up by steps unto mine altar, that thy nakedness be not uncovered thereon" (Ex. 20:26). God's principle is that no exposure is permitted. Other than the hands, feet, and head—which are covered by the blood—all the rest of the body must be clothed. The modern trend to expose more and more of the body violates God's original thought.

CLOTHING OF THE PRIESTS

The clothes that the priests wore were made with fine needlework allowing no spaces between, for the priests were not permitted to expose themselves before God. The robes of the ephod which they wore were especially long, and their linen breeches reached from the loin to the thighs (Ex. 28:42). The Bible consistently maintains the rule of having the body covered, not exposed.

REPRESENTATIVE MEANING

God uses clothes to represent both the Lord Jesus Himself and the redemption we obtain from Him. We are clothed with God's salvation, we are clothed with Christ, and we are clothed with the new man. We are clothed, so much clothed that our entire beings are covered; there are no holes.

Lead new believers to understand that when they put their clothes on, they should see beyond those clothes to Christ and His salvation. "Thank God," they may muse, "I was formerly as one naked, void of any covering before God, unable to escape God's light and His judgment; but today I am clothed with the salvation of God, with the new man." From the clothes which cover them completely, new believers can see how they are fully covered in God's sight. How wonderful that we are wholly covered before God.

The rule for clothing is to cover. If it does not cover, a Christian should not wear it. Clothes which expose rather than cover should not be used. They are against the principle of covering and therefore are unsuitable for Christians.

2. LEPROSY

In Leviticus we are told that garments, as well as people and houses, can be plagued with leprosy. Much of today's clothing, especially women's dresses, has this plague of leprosy.

TWO TREATMENTS

We find in Leviticus 13 that there are two different ways to treat a garment attacked by leprosy. As the priest examines such a garment, if he finds the plague has spread, he orders the garment burned for it has a fretting leprosy. If the plague does not spread, he orders the leprous part rent out of the warp or the woof and then the garment washed. If the plague still does not spread, he has the garment washed a second time; then it is clean. But if the plague spreads, he orders the garment burned.

ASK GOD

New brothers and sisters who have never had any experience in this matter should take note. You may have some doubt about some of your clothes, whether or not you can wear them. Why not bring them to the Lord? He is our High Priest. Ask Him to show you whether you may wear them. Do not think such a matter is too small. For new believers, especially for sisters, clothes are a big problem. Others cannot tell you which clothes have the plague of leprosy and which do not. You must yourself bring them to the Lord in order to know.

Remember: the person with leprosy must go away; the house with leprosy must be wrecked; and the garment with leprosy must be burned. Some clothing, after alterations such as lengthening the sleeves, changing the style somewhat, or dyeing to a different color, can still be used. Others, even after alterations, still seem to have the plague in them. Consequently they must be gotten rid of. New believers should bring their clothes one by one to the Lord to examine and deal with.

I hope that when brothers and sisters go out they may be recognized as Christians. I do not expect their clothing to cast doubts upon their Christian profession. By your clothes men shall judge whether or not you are a Christian. Let not a clean person wear a garment with the plague of leprosy. Since you have already had your leprosy cleansed and your sins forgiven, you should not again wear a garment with leprosy on it.

Let us lead new believers to bring their clothes one by one to the Lord in prayer over them. Other believers should not tell them which clothes can be used and which cannot. Do not criticize their dress. Bring them to the Lord instead, and let them bring their clothes to Him. They should ask the Lord directly which clothes are suitable for believers and which are not. Some clothes they may have to get rid of; others they may keep after alterations. Let the Lord teach the new believers what to do. They themselves must decide which clothes are sinful for them. May they solve this problem well.

3. MEN'S AND WOMEN'S CLOTHING

"A woman shall not wear that which pertaineth unto a man, neither shall a man put on a woman's garment; for whosoever doeth these things is an abomination unto Jehovah thy God" (Deut. 22:5). Thus the Bible forbids a man wearing a woman's garment or a woman a man's. The tendency today is to blur the distinction between men's and women's clothing until there is none. Hence, brothers and sisters must be careful not to wear clothing indiscriminately. We must maintain God's appointed distinction—man wears man's clothing and woman wears woman's dress. Any attempt to confuse this distinction is dishonoring to the Lord. The children of God ought to learn how to dress before God; they should keep the distinction between man and woman in clothing.

4. THE SISTERS' PROBLEM

Ordinarily brothers have less problem with clothing than sisters have.

BEAUTIFUL APPAREL AND MEEKNESS

"Whose adorning let it not be the outward adorning of braiding the hair, and of wearing jewels of gold, or of putting on apparel; but let it be the hidden man of the heart, in the incorruptible apparel of a meek and quiet spirit, which is in the sight of God of great price" (1 Pet. 3:3-4). If I remember correctly, the next verse (verse five) is the only occurrence in the Bible of the term "holy women." There are many places where "holy men" is used, but here we have "holy women." "For after this manner aforetime the holy women also, who hoped in God, adorned themselves, being in subjection to their own husbands Holy women adorned themselves with a meek and quiet spirit.

What Peter means is that while sisters would quite naturally adorn themselves with braiding of hair, wearing of jewels, and putting on of beautiful apparel, many of these hairdos, jewels, and apparel are not too suitable. I think we need to emphasize here that this does not in any wise suggest that a sister may be careless in her clothing. If she is neglectful in her manner of dressing, not neat and clean, then her manner of life must unavoidably be careless and loose. This betrays a defective character.

"Braiding the hair" in the original Greek means to

fashion the hair in many ways. We know how women throughout the centuries have invented many styles of hairdo. "Jewels of gold" refers to wearing jewels for adornment. "Apparel" or "beautiful apparel" may be related to color or to fashion. Peter stresses that sisters should not make these their outward adorning; rather, they should be adorned with the incorruptible quality of a meek and quiet spirit.

It is unfitting for a woman to be gorgeously dressed and yet display the temper of a lioness. There is no consistency in seeing a beautifully robed woman shouting and raging. If a woman is meek and quiet, she will be reckoned as clothed in splendor. A sister who serves God should not be too much occupied with her clothing; we Christians should not be overly attentive to what we wear.

PROPER CLOTHING WITH MODESTY
AND DISCRETION

"In like manner, that women adorn themselves in modest apparel, with shamefastness and sobriety; not with braided hair, and gold or pearls or costly raiment; but (which becometh women professing godliness) through good works. Let a woman learn in quietness and with all subjection" (1 Tim. 2:9–11).

God has a basic requirement for the sisters, and that is, they should possess the sense of modesty or shamefacedness. It is good for sisters to feel ashamed, for it is their natural protection. Do not wear what is against your sense of modesty. "Sobriety" is the opposite of looseness. Be sober in the way you dress; do not wear indecent clothes. We may not know exactly what "modest apparel" or "proper clothing" is, but every sister knows what will be considered modest in the area where she lives. A Christian must not be so dressed as to be thought inappropriate by the unbelievers. Our standard should not be lower than the unbelievers. We need to learn what shamefacedness is, how to be sober, and what modest dress is.

"Braided hair" here points especially to curling the hair as in making many curls like bunches of grapes. Actually, two thousand years ago women already made such curls. "Costly garments" refers to the price of the material. Two dresses may be similar but cost different amounts. The style may be the same, but the materials are different. People like to wear costly apparel. Since the use is the same, we should not waste money on costly dresses. Sisters ought to dress modestly. Neither Peter nor Paul nor we ourselves mean in the slightest that a sister should be carelessly or negligently dressed. We only assert that sisters ought not to go for costly raiment but should be dressed in modesty. It is best for a sister to manage to attire herself neatly in ordinary material at a common price. I have seen some sisters spend too much time and money on beautiful, costly raiment, and I have also noticed many sisters pay no attention as to whether they are neatly and cleanly dressed. A woman's clothing is especially important because it represents her character.

5. THE SEAL OF THE HOLY SPIRIT

"And Moses took of the anointing oil, and of the blood which was upon the altar, and sprinkled it upon Aaron, upon his garments, and upon his sons, and upon his sons' garments with him, and sanctified Aaron, his garments, and his sons, and his sons' garments with him" (Lev. 8:30). Our garments must be sanctified; the mark of the anointing oil, the seal of the Holy Spirit, needs to be upon them. Even as we are holy in person, we ought to be clothed in a holy manner. Both the man and his garments were anointed with oil and sanctified together.

"And Jehovah spake unto Moses, saying, Speak unto the children of Israel, and bid them that they make them fringes in the borders of their garments throughout their generations, and that they put upon the fringe of each border a cord of blue" (Num. 15:37–38). Blue is the color of the sky; it is to remind us of heavenly things. The clothing of believers should have a heavenly taste to it. Do not imitate the world in its careless way nor in its excessive manner. We should exhibit a heavenly mode which proves that both we and our garments are sanctified.

6. SOME PERSONAL OBSERVATIONS

PERSONAL FREEDOM

I would like to make a few personal observations on the matter of clothing. I do not believe that all children of God must dress alike, nor am I of the opinion that sisters should disregard beauty or that all brothers and sisters should be clothed with only the most common and cheapest materials. The Bible never endorses such a thought. John the Baptist came with raiment of camel's hair, whereas the Lord Jesus came with a seamless coat—the best of that time. So, as a basic principle, a Christian is free to dress as he likes, free to choose what material he prefers, and free to wear the style he likes.

BE INCONSPICUOUS

We have liberty to dress as we like, but I think we need to notice one thing: no one should be so attired as to divert people's attention to his clothes instead of to himself. If

162

such a thing happens, something is wrong with the apparel. The clothes I wear ought to manifest me. If I make a flower arrangement and friends notice only the vase and not the flowers, something is wrong with the vase. Clothing is to help people know me, not to usurp my place. It is a big mistake, nay, a terrible thing if one is so clothed that people notice the clothes but not the person.

BE SUITABLY DRESSED

Another thing to be noticed is that a person should be dressed according to his individual prerogative, that is, relevant to his particular privilege or position. Do not be clothed out of one's station in life or occupation; to be too well or too poorly dressed will arouse others' attention. This is what we must avoid. Let us therefore be clothed as becomes our prerogative. Thus we shall glorify the Lord

AVOID SELF-CONSCIOUSNESS

Brothers and sisters should not be so clothed as to make themselves conscious of what they wear. If one is aware all the time of his dress, whether it be too good or too poor, something is definitely wrong with that dress. He has become a clothes hanger, for his clothes have assumed a more important role than he has. The clothes are wearing him instead of him wearing the clothes!

It is best, therefore, to wear clothes which make neither you nor others aware of them. They should be ordinary and yet becoming to a Christian. They should agree with your station in life.

Do not think it is a small thing to be dressed like a Christian; it affects our testimony before the world.

Eating

Let us now turn to eating.

The need for food existed before the fall of man. So, in Genesis 2, God gave food to man. (Clothing, however, did not become a need until Genesis 3.) Before man sinned, God already gave all kinds of fruit for man's food. God ordained that man should eat fruit.

1. THE NEED

After man sinned in Genesis 3, God gave him the herb of the field to eat, but it was only in the sweat of his face that he would eat bread Though nothing was explicitly said about food in Genesis 4, yet the seal of God was upon Abel, not on Cain. Cain was a farmer, while Abel was a shepherd. God's seal was on Abel, because God accepted his offering. Cain offered the produce of his field to God, but he was not accepted. We do not know what God might be implying in Genesis 4, but when we come to Genesis 9 we see that God clearly gave the animals to man for food, even as formerly He had given him the fruits of the trees.

LIFE FROM DEATH

Why does God give the flesh of the beast of the earth to man for food? Because man obviously is in need of such food. The kind of food man needed before and after he sinned was not the same. Food is that which maintains life. Without eating, man cannot live. Without food he cannot continue on the earth. For the sake of keeping man alive, God has ordained that man should eat the flesh of animals as well as the herbs of the field and fruits. In other words, God is showing that since sin has entered into the world, the losing of life is required to preserve life. The animals must lose their life in order to maintain our life. Before sin entered into the world life could be sustained without the shedding of blood. Hence there is a difference in the food provision for man before and after sin. Christians today, living after sin entered, should not be vegetarians; they should eat meat.

We are not now discussing the benefit meat has for our physical bodies. We leave this to those engaged in medical research; it is generally recognized that animal protein is better than vegetable protein. But we have a basic principle here: after man sinned, there can be no life without death. Life can only be sustained by death. Without death man cannot live. The shedding of blood keeps him alive.

Starting first with Abel, then clearly manifested after the flood, God has outlined for men this matter of eating meat. By being a vegetarian man unwittingly declares that he can live without death, without the shedding of blood. By eating meat, however, man acknowledges that without death and the shedding of blood he is unable to live. Have you seen this principle? This is why God gives the flesh of the beasts of the earth to man for food. Man has to depend on the losing of life in order to live. Thank God, another has lost life that we might gain life.

At the time of Romans 14 some people still thought they could eat vegetables only, just as in the day of Adam. Paul told people not to criticize them nor hinder them. Those who ate meat should not judge the ones who did not, and vice versa. Nevertheless, Paul also pointed out that the vegetarians were the weak ones (v. 2). In consideration of their weakness, they were not to be criticized; but this did not imply that their eating only herbs was right. It simply meant that others should not trouble them for the sake of food.

Nevertheless, we must know that according to Christian redemption, life comes out of death. *In order to have life there must first be death.* Vegetables alone cannot give life. Life is maintained through death. If a person's conscience is weak so that he eats only herbs, we should refrain from touching his weakness. But Christianity affirms that meat is for the maintenance of life.

A DOCTRINE OF DEMONS

"But the Spirit saith expressly, that in later times some shall fall away from the faith, giving heed to seducing spirits and doctrines of demons . . . forbidding to marry, and commanding to abstain from meats [food]" (1 Tim. 4:1, 3). I think the comment of D. M. Panton on this passage sheds clear light. He said that forbidding to marry and abstaining from meats were aids to developing the soulical power. We do not advocate abstaining from meats, for this is the doctrine of demons and not of the Lord. Some practice abstaining from meats because they are ignorant of Christian principle. The Christian principle is *to gain life out of death.* If one eats only herbs and no meat, he unknowingly is saying that since his life can be maintained by herbs, he has no need for the Savior, neither His death nor His salvation. Therefore, new believers must be instructed in this matter.

2. BLOOD FORBIDDEN

There *is* one thing a Christian should not eat, and that is, blood.

CLOTHING AND EATING

THROUGHOUT THE BIBLE

From the Old Testament to the New Testament, the teaching against eating blood is consistent. In Genesis 9 God spoke to Noah saying, "the blood thereof, shall ye not eat" (v. 4). Eating blood is forbidden by God.

In Leviticus 17:10–16 God reiterated many times, "Ye shall eat the blood of no manner of flesh; for the life of all flesh is the blood thereof: whosoever eateth it shall be cut off" (v. 14). God will not recognize as being His own that soul who eats blood.

In the New Testament, at the first council in Jerusalem (Acts 15), the church was faced with a great difficulty concerning the law. James, Peter, Paul, Barnabas and other servants of God decided together that God's children should not be burdened with keeping the law; only they should abstain from things sacrificed to idols, and from blood, and from things strangled, and from fornication.

Thus the importance of the blood is evident. At the time of the patriarchs, God forbade the eating of blood through Noah; under the law, He forbade the same through Moses; in the dispensation of grace, He forbade again through the apostles. In all three dispensations, God said no.

EXCEPT THE BLOOD OF CHRIST

One day the Son of God came to the world. He stated that He is the bread come down out of heaven which gives life to the world. Many did not understand His meaning. So He explained by saying, "For my flesh is meat indeed, and my blood is drink indeed" (John 6:55). In the sixth chapter of the Gospel according to John, the Lord repeated this same thought many times in different ways, such as, "Except ye eat the flesh of the Son of man and drink his blood, ye have not life in yourselves. He that eateth my flesh and drinketh my blood hath eternal life; and I will raise him up at the last day" (vv. 53–54).

Indeed, this is rather marvelous. In all three dispensations, the Bible forbids the eating of blood; yet Jesus of Nazareth, the Son of God, declares that His blood may be drunk. Do you see God's way here? God forbids us to eat all kinds of blood, but he who drinks of the blood of the Lord is saved. There is only one kind of blood which we may drink. After drinking the blood of the Lord, we should not drink any other blood.

In other words, through the prohibition of eating blood, God tells us that there is only one redemption, one salvation. Apart from this one redemption, there is none other. Apart from this one salvation, none other is given. The blood of Jesus of Nazareth is the only blood that is drinkable. All other blood is undrinkable, for only the blood of Jesus represents redemption, it stands for salvation. We therefore refuse any other blood; we reject any other salvation. Apart from the salvation of Jesus Christ, we know no other salvation. We have only one blood, not two bloods. This blood alone can save us; others we refuse.

Young believers need to be instructed that, small as this matter may seem, it yet contains a testimony. We Christians have many ways to testify, and this is one of them. When unbelievers ask us why we do not eat blood, our answer is: we have already eaten. We can show them what salvation is. By not eating blood, we are able to give a strong testimony before men. We do not eat because we have already eaten. Since we have eaten, we cannot eat any other blood. The blood of Jesus of Nazareth is our only salvation; therefore we reject any other blood.

168

The Old Testament, including Leviticus 17, mentions that dead things should not be eaten. Here in Acts 15, it says strangled things must not be eaten. This is also for the sake of blood, because when strangled things are cooked whole, the blood is not separated from the flesh. By not eating blood, we maintain that in none other is there salvation but in that of the Lord Jesus Christ.

3. THE QUESTION OF CLEAN OR UNCLEAN

In Leviticus 11 God told the Israelites that some beasts on the earth were clean and some unclean, some eatable and some not eatable. This was also true of the birds of the air and the fish of the sea: birds that were carnivorous were not to be eaten; fish without fins and scales should also not be eaten.

The question may be asked: what is the significance of these ordinances in Leviticus 11? Should we believers keep them? This will lead us to Acts 10. Peter was praying upon the housetop; he fell into a trance and saw the heaven opened. A certain vessel descended, "as it were a great sheet, let down by four corners upon the earth: wherein were all manner of fourfooted beasts and creeping things of the earth and birds of the heaven" (Acts 10:11–12). These were the uneatable things of Leviticus 11. God asked Peter to rise up, kill, and eat. Being a good Jew, Peter answered that he had never eaten anything unclean. The voice spoke a second time to him, saying, "What God has cleansed, make not thou common." And this was done three times.

A MATTER OF ELECTION

We now understand that what is said in Leviticus 11 is actually to enunciate the teaching of Acts 10. Was God really interested in what fish may be eaten and what may not? Was it possible that God had not thought of this matter when He first gave all fish to Noah as food? At that time, all beasts of the earth could be taken as food; there was no distinction between the clean and the unclean. Why, then, is this question of clean or unclean raised in Leviticus 11? It is because at the time of Noah God had not yet chosen His own people on the earth. But the time of Leviticus was the time during which God elected Israel. In leading them out of Egypt, God chose Israel as His people. There came into being a distinction between God's people and not God's people. The question of clean or unclean, which formed no problem at Noah's time, had become a problem by the time of Leviticus. Ever since then, there have been Jews and Gentiles, God's people and not God's people. Only since the time of Leviticus has there been a distinction between the clean and the unclean, the eatable and the uneatable. It points to that which may be fellowshiped and that which may not; between that which is acceptable to God and that which is not. Food carries with it a representative value. Food is more than food, it embodies a principle. What is eatable is what God desires; what is not eatable is what God rejects.

GRACE UPON THE GENTILES

After the baptism in the Holy Spirit on the day of Pentecost, God said to Peter, "Rise, kill and eat." From then on, the grace of God came upon the unclean Gentiles. Today anyone may be chosen. What God reckoned as unclean in the Old Testament, He considers clean in the New Testament. The prohibition of Leviticus 11 is no longer in effect. No longer are only the Israelites God's people; both the Gentiles and the Israelites are now the people of God. According to Ephesians 3, the Jews and the Gentiles are made one, being "fellow-heirs, and fellow-members of the body, and fellow partakers of the promise in Christ Jesus through the gospel" (v. 6).

God spoke to Peter three times: "What God hath cleansed, make not thou common." These words explain the vision. As soon as the vision ceased, the men from the house of Cornelius the Gentile knocked at the door. As he went down to meet them, Peter began to understand that what he had seen on the housetop meant that God was going to give grace to the Gentiles. So, without hesitation, he took some brothers with him to the house of a Gentile. Later, he testified that God manifestly gave grace to the Gentiles even as He had to the Jews.

JEWISH AND CHRISTIAN TESTIMONY DIFFERENT

Our testimony differs from that of the Jews. We maintain that as the Jews are the people of God, so today the Gentiles are God's people. If we refrain from eating certain things, we would be acting as if the Jews alone are God's people and we are not. No, the order for today is to rise, kill, and eat. No distinction is to be made between the clean and the unclean. What God has cleansed, none should make common.

Consequently, new believers should realize that by eating both the so-called clean and unclean, they testify that both Jews and Gentiles are God's people. We are not called to maintain Leviticus 11; rather, today we are to bear witness to the fact that the Jews and the Gentiles are fellow-heirs of grace, that there is no difference. Thus we affirm this testimony through our way of eating.

4. THINGS SACRIFICED TO IDOLS

The first letter to the Corinthians has a great deal to say about things sacrificed to idols. In the eighth chapter Paul tells us that an idol is nothing, for God alone is God. According to the highest knowledge, it is nothing to eat things sacrificed to idols because idols are nothing. There may be evil spirits behind the idols, but God is greater than the evil spirits. He Who dwells in us is much greater than he that is in the world.

Nevertheless, many new believers in the past worshiped idols in the temples, being ignorant at that time of what communion with demons meant. Now, having come to the Lord, when they see those eating in the temple who know idols are nothing, they conclude that they can do the same. Their conduct is the same as those who know, but their understanding is very different. These with knowledge go and eat because they know idols are nothing; whereas those who formerly worshiped idols eat as of things sacrificed to idols. Thus they stumble into sin through the carelessness of the strong.

For this reason, Paul concludes that it is better for us believers not to eat things sacrificed to idols, lest we become a stumbling block to the weak. In reference to vegetarianism, Paul says it is the weak who eat only herbs. But as to things sacrificed to idols, Paul says it is better not to eat. The underlying principle here is the conscience of the weak. We do not eat things sacrificed to idols, not because of the demon but because of the brothers. We are fearful lest they be stumbled, though we ourselves have no fear. Satan has no power in us; idols have no influence over us. Though we are not afraid of demons, yet we must learn before God not to stumble our brothers through our eating.

5. SOME PERSONAL OBSERVATIONS

Finally, I would like to express some of my opinions.

FOOD FOR NOURISHMENT

Ordinarily the principle of eating is the nourishment of the physical body. Therefore, eat what is nourishing and do not eat what does not nourish. Never make the belly your god; do not be too much occupied with food. We as God's children should know that eating is for the sake of nourishing the body and preserving physical life.

CONTENTMENT AND GOD'S ADDITION

God's children should remember that "having food and covering we shall be therewith content" (1 Tim. 6:8). "Behold the birds of the heaven, that they sow not, neither do they reap, nor gather into barns; and your heavenly Father feedeth them" (Matt. 6:26). "Consider the lilies of the field, how they grow; they toil not, neither do they spin: yet I say unto you, that even Solomon in all his glory was not arrayed like one of these" (Matt. 6:28). Verse 26 is in reference to eating, but verse 28 to clothing. All is in God's hand. "Seek ye first his kingdom, and his righteousness; and all these things shall be added unto you" (Matt. 6:33; see the whole passage of Matt. 6:25–33). I like the word "added." What does it mean? Let me ask this question, How much is three added to zero? You would remonstrate with me saying, "Three cannot be added to zero for no amount can be added to zero. This is an impossible question; there is no need to add three to zero." What, then, can be added? You can add to something already there, such as add three to one. Seek the kingdom of God and His righteousness, and all these things shall be added to you. To those who possess God's kingdom and His righteousness, He will add food and clothing. May all brothers and sisters remember well that God's kingdom and His righteousness is what we seek. All who have gained the kingdom of God are those who live in the righteousness of God. To them shall these things be added.

May God's children know how to maintain their testimony among men in these two respects of clothing and eating.

ASCETICISM

The Origin of Asceticism

Before a person is saved, he quite naturally has some sort of an ideal. Though he has fallen into sin, he still has a standard. There is a certain kind of life that he considers holy. If he could reach this standard, he would have a holy life. Is this not a strange thing, that though many unbelievers live a life full of sin and lust, they nonetheless do hold an ideal of what holy living is? They think that if they were some day to arrive at such a state, they would be holy and noble!

1. OF THE WORLD

After we are saved, we too easily bring this concept of holiness into the church. We surmise that the ideal life we failed to arrive at in the past can now be reached, for now we are Christians. Formerly we lived in sin and lust; we had no strength to overcome the weakness of our flesh. Now that we have believed in the Lord, we are well able to live our ideal life. However, in such thinking there is a basic difficulty: people forget that *this ideal is of the world; it*

175

is not a Christian ideal. The standard of too many Christians is their own standard; oftentimes it is the same as that of unbelievers. Their ideal life is the ideal of unbelievers. They have simply transferred their former philosophy into the church. Because of this, it is necessary that new believers be made clear on this point.

2. FULL OF LUST, YET WANTING DELIVERANCE

What is the ideal life to which man ascribes? Often it is based on the very thing which he himself cannot do. While under the bondage of sin, lust, and evil desires, man cherishes the thought of transcending, yet finds he is utterly powerless. Though he loves material things, he nevertheless respects those who can transcend these things. The more he is bound by a certain thing, the more he admires those who are free of it. The stronger his lust, the greater his aspiration for deliverance from that lust. The more he covets material things, the deeper his longing to be freed from them. It is for this reason that people of the world hold to a kind of ascetic concept. Remember, asceticism is not meant for people of the world to follow; it merely supplies them with an ideal. With this ideal people may comfort themselves. At the least, they have a goal, and with this goal they can conveniently forget their present condition. They keep telling themselves that if they could arrive at the goal, they would be at the summit. Such is the origin of asceticism.

Most unbelievers seek to fulfill the lust of the flesh yet in their hearts admire those who are free from such things. They wish that they too might be delivered from the bondage of material things. Hence, asceticism is their ideal; it is the upward look of those who are outside Christ.

Asceticism Not Found in Christianity

After one believes in the Lord, he may unconsciously carry asceticism into the church. In the past, though he might not have practiced it, he admired the ascetics. At the same time that he respected the ascetic, though, the unbeliever usually was also materialistic. So it is very easy for him to carry his admiration for asceticism into Christianity along with the thought that now he will really practice asceticism.

1. DESPISES MATERIAL THINGS AND SUPPRESSES PASSIONS

What is really meant by asceticism? To many people asceticism means the prohibition of material things. The less material things they use, the better they are. This is because they fear that these external things will fill their passions and lusts. The ascetic person acknowledges that within man there are lusts and passions. He realizes that from the lust for food to the lust for sex, all sorts of lusts are inherent in man. Each lust is shared and indulged in by the people of the world. If anyone desires to be a holy man, he must conquer these lusts and passions. Therefore, asceticism is outwardly despising material things and inwardly suppressing lusts and passions.

2. NOT ADVOCATED BY CHRISTIANITY

New believers need to be shown that Christianity never advocates asceticism. How superficial Christianity would be if this were what it stood for.

We hope that by studying a little more of the Bible, we may see what asceticism really is; nothing more than an attempt to suppress oneself in food and drink, in lusts and passions, and in other material things. This is not Christianity, nor is it the ideal Christian life. As a matter of fact, the Bible never endorses asceticism.

Dead to the Philosophy of the World

"If ye died with Christ from the rudiments of the world, why, as though living in the world, do ye subject yourselves to ordinances, Handle not, nor taste, nor touch (all which things are to perish with the using), after the precepts and doctrines of men? Which things have indeed a show of wisdom in will-worship, and humility, and severity to the body; but are not of any value against the indulgence of the flesh" (Col. 2:20–23). "Rudiments" in verse 20 should be translated as "philosophy."

1. CO-DEATH WITH CHRIST

When Paul writes to the believers at Colosse "if ye died with Christ," he takes this as a fundamental Christian fact. We who are Christians *have* died with Christ. The whole New Testament shows us that every Christian has died with Christ. Romans 6 informs us that "our old man was crucified with him" (v. 6). Galatians 2 states categorically that "I have been crucified with Christ" (v. 20). In the same letter, it affirms that "they that are of Christ Jesus have crucified the flesh with the passions and the lusts thereof" (5:24). The Bible teaches that we Christians were crucified with Christ. In other words, the cross of Calvary is the Christian's cross; the cross of Christ is the Christian's cross. The starting point for a Christian is the cross, not just the cross of Christ but one's own cross too. As we receive the cross of Christ, His cross becomes our cross. He who has not accepted the fact of the cross is not a

Christian. To him who has become a Christian, the cross of Christ has also become a fact—that is, he has died in Christ.

To Paul, the fact of the cross of Christ was beyond doubt. He based whatever he had to say on this fact. He reasoned that once you have died with Christ, there will be some necessary consequences. It is as sure as if we say to brother Ting who sits here, "Is your name Ting? Is the fact that you are Mr. Ting indisputable? If so, I want to talk to you on the basis of this sure fact so that whatever I say will be unassailable." In other words, whatever conclusion Paul draws for us is based on the fact of our having died with Christ.

2. NOT THE PHILOSOPHY OF THE WORLD

"If ye have died with Christ from the rudiments [philosophy] of the world." No one in the grave can be a philosopher. If anyone desires to talk philosophy, he must do so while he is living. For us, however, philosophy is already dead on the cross. This matter has already been fully resolved, for the philosophy of the world postulates that holiness may be attained by abandoning material things and suppressing one's inner lusts and passions. Paul, however, says that if you have died with Christ from the philosophy of the world, you are no longer involved with such philosophical jargon.

3. NOT AS LIVING IN THE WORLD

"If ye have died with Christ from the philosophy of the world," Paul asks, "why [do you act] as though living in the world?" If death is a fact, you cannot live like the people of the world. The basic position of a Christian is death.

179

Ask a new believer why he was baptized if it were not that he is dead. Man must be dead before he is buried; otherwise he would be buried alive. A person is baptized because he has been crucified with Christ; therefore he is buried. Co-death is already a fact, but burial is something yet to be done. The Lord has already included the new believer in His death; now, as declared in the burial of baptism, the believer *sees* that he is dead. Knowing now of his death, he asks to be buried. So, having believed and been baptized, having died and been buried, how can he again be as though living in the world?

Through Paul, we can see that those who practice asceticism are still living in the world. Hence Paul says, "Why, as though living in the world, do ye subject yourselves to ordinances, Handle not, nor taste, nor touch?" According to ascetic teaching, there are things which should not be tasted or eaten, handled or even touched. Such ordinances originate from the fear of man's inward passions and lusts. At the time Paul wrote, asceticism was flourishing in Colosse. Many ordinances were practiced by the Colossians. Lest their lusts be stirred, they prohibited the use of all things which might incite the passions. There were some things they were not to handle, others they were not to touch, others they could not taste, and others they could not hear. By these strict ordinances, they hoped to keep material things separated from passions and lusts. The philosophical concept of those days was that by such separation lust was controlled.

Paul, however, remonstrates that to be subject to such ordinances is to not believe in the fact of being crucified with Christ. If you believe you have died, should there, then, be such prohibitions? Only a person who is alive can practice the ordinances of handle not, touch not, and taste not. Asceticism has its claim only on the living, not on the dead.

Remember, all who are of Christ Jesus *have* crucified the flesh with its passions and lusts. If you bind yourself by the human concept of fleeing from matter and lust, you are not standing on Christian ground; you have not taken the ground of death. No one can be a Christian without death, without having died with Christ. Make no mistake on this point.

Although we have been preaching co-death, there will be many who still do not understand what it is. This is because co-death is a fact, not a doctrine. It is set before us as an already accomplished fact. Yet many are still seeking to die with Christ. We need to see that co-death is our starting point, not our ending point. The mystic looks at co-death as a goal to pursue, but this is not the Christian teaching. Unless we are dead with Christ, we cannot be Christians. To seek to die with Christ is an act of folly, clearly showing a lack of light. One who has light and meets the truth of co-death will praise, not pursue. It is the same as seeing the substitutionary death of the Lord Jesus; it too sets our hearts to praising instead of pursuing.

Paul's basic teaching is that the Christian has already died with Christ; hence, he has also been delivered from the philosophy of the world and from its ordinances. We may illustrate it this way: if a thief has been buried in a tomb, you may stand by that tomb and declare with confidence that that thief will never again steal. He who is dead is freed from stealing. Likewise, you may be a very talkative person, but having died with Christ, you are delivered from talkativeness. Asceticism is of no help to those who have died; it comes too late, for they already have been crucified with Christ.

181

4. Not the Precepts and Doctrines of Men

"After the precepts and doctrines of men." All these ordinances, all these ascetic requirements, only follow the precepts of men. They are a product of the human mind. They are of man and are not related to Christ and His church. People may say, I should not eat this, I should not touch that. But let us remember, these are man's commandments, man's teachings. They are not God's.

Paul's conclusion, when he categorically states that these are the commandments and teachings of men, is serious. His conclusion is that man's ideal of life, being built on human concepts and ordinances, is totally unrelated to God. Surprisingly, the world relishes asceticism. It seems noble for one not to eat and drink what ordinary people do. Such a one must be pure to be so free of the material things which entangle others. Take note that asceticism is natural religion, not revealed Christianity. Natural religion follows the precepts and doctrines of men wherein there is neither light nor revelation, only the human reaction against passion and lust. Indeed, asceticism shows how deeply man knows that his passions and lusts are defiling.

5. Asceticism Is Unworkable

How does Paul judge the effectiveness of asceticism? "All which things are to perish with the using." Asceticism is pleasant to listen to, and it sounds well as a philosophy to talk about. But if you try to use it, it is like a car which looks fine in the garage but always stalls on the street. Or it may be likened to a dress which looks beautiful in the closet but is found to be full of holes when put on the body. If you try asceticism, you will see it is unable to help you get rid of your evil lusts and passions.

The more you prohibit yourself, the more things you find within you. The more you flee, the more obvious the fear of your heart becomes. I have met a few of the world's so-called sages. I can testify that you may detect in their conversation that they are not free from the lusts and passions they are trying to escape or hide from all the time. Their hard fleeing is proof of the depth of their consciousness. Many flee to the wilderness and sequester themselves from contact with the world, because its power is so great upon them. But the world follows them to the mountains as well as to the wilderness. Due to the lack of victory within, there is no escaping without. How well Paul concludes, "all which things are to perish with the using." They have no way to be delivered from their lusts and passions. When their lusts are stirred, they collapse. In trying to be separated from the world and delivered from their lusts, they set up many ordinances; but, as a matter of fact, they find that these things of the world remain with them. Is not their fear a reflection of the hold these things have upon them?

6. Asceticism Is a Show of Wisdom

"Which things have indeed a show of wisdom in will-worship" (v. 23). These advocates of asceticism are the world's wise people. They seem to be full of wisdom; they certainly can talk convincingly. Many people esteem them wise.

7. Asceticism Is Will-Worship

Paul judges asceticism as will-worship. The ordinances which are set up belong to the worship of the ascetic, not to the worship of the Lord. God is Spirit, and those who worship Him must worship Him in spirit. The ascetics have no spirit (their human spirits are dead to God), so they use their wills to control themselves. Theirs is a will-religion. *Will-worship is will-religion,* for this religion is the product of the will: I will not taste, I will not touch, I will not handle. It is all "I." It is the will which causes one to worship. In other words, it is a will-religion.

Remember, this is not our Christian way. The Christian way is to contact God with the spirit. We are characterized not by suppressing lusts with our will but by touching the Spirit of God with our strong spirits. Our spirit touching God's Spirit—this is our worship. The Christian way is purely of God; the ascetic way is wholly of man.

8. ASCETICISM IS MANUFACTURED HUMILITY

"Which things have indeed a show of . . . humility" (v. 23). Even humility in asceticism is self-manufactured. It gives an appearance of self-abasement in that one does not touch or taste or handle many things. But such humility comes from one's self; it is man-made. It is a self-created humility, not the spontaneously spiritual humility.

9. ASCETICISM IS SELF-MORTIFICATION

"Which things have indeed a show of . . . severity to the body" (v. 23). The attitude of ascetics toward themselves is severity to the body. They take no care how they eat or clothe themselves; they deny their bodies in seeing, touching, hearing, and handling. Such a life gives them an appearance of being humble; actually it is nothing other than self-mortification.

The ascetic reckons the body as defiled. This concept started in ancient Greece and spread to India and to China. Of course, not all ancient Greeks practiced asceticism, but there was one school that taught that the body is the root of all evil. According to their teaching, if one can be delivered from the body he is freed from sin. This later became a basic tenet in Buddhism. According to this philosophy, the human body is the source of sin. Since it can produce so many sins, the body ought to be afflicted. Physical affliction will decrease the amount one sins. Such is human religion, the religion of the world. Men always generalize that it is right to make the body suffer. Deprive the body of enjoyment, cause it to suffer. The more afflicted it is the better, for then the soul will not sin.

10. ASCETICISM OF NO VALUE

From the standpoint of believers, such efforts "are not of any value against the indulgence of the flesh." The Lord Jesus on the cross has already prepared for us a more excellent provision—by having our flesh with its passions and lusts crucified. Today our stand is found in the cross; we apply the finished work of the cross upon the passions and lusts of our flesh. How different this is from man's way of dealing with lusts and passions! The Christian acknowledges the fact of the cross of Christ.

In the same manner as people receive forgiveness of sins through the shedding of the blood of the Lord Jesus, so are they delivered from lusts through the cross of the Lord Jesus. The shedding of blood and the cross are both the works of Christ. Immediately after we accept the blood and the cross, we should be baptized. Because the Lord has already crucified *us*, therefore we must be buried. The meaning of baptism is that the Lord says I am dead; so I say I will be buried. The Lord says I have been crucified and therefore I no longer live. I say I have no doubt about this death and hence ask to be buried. Baptism is the expression of our acceptance of the death of the Lord

Jesus. But the practice of asceticism is a denial of this ground of death.

11. SEEK THE THINGS ABOVE

"If then ye were raised together with Christ, seek the things that are above, where Christ is, seated on the right hand of God. Set your mind on the things that are above, not on the things that are upon the earth. For ye died, and your life is hid with Christ in God" (Col. 3:1–3). Paul begins with the cross and concludes with resurrection. He says that since we are a heavenly people, we should not mind the things that are upon the earth. If we stress these things (touch not, taste not, handle not), we are yet thinking of earthly things. But we are resurrected, and as resurrected people we should seek the things that are above. By minding heavenly things, these earthly problems will automatically be solved. Let us, then, as Christians, think of the heavenly things; let us not think of such things as taste not, touch not, and handle not.

Asceticism Is a Doctrine of Demons

Another reason we Christians do not advocate asceticism is because it is an error introduced into Christianity from heathenism. So we must deal with it thoroughly.

"But the Spirit saith expressly, that in later times some shall fall away from the faith, giving heed to seducing spirits and doctrines of demons . . . forbidding to marry, and commanding to abstain from meats" (1 Tim. 4:1, 3). Toward the end of this age, asceticism will be greatly revived. The present generation may be materialistically inclined, but the next generation will have a reaction against materialism and will endorse asceticism. What

186

does asceticism do? It forbids marriage and meat. It is an attempt to take away sex and food.

Urge and Lust Differ

We Christians need to know the difference between a natural urge and lust. Let us explain these two briefly.

1. URGE

When God decided that we should eat, He gave us the urge for food. At that time, this urge for food was neither sinful nor lustful. Because of this urge, man eats and thus preserves his life. God delights in seeing man preserve his life, so He gives him an urge that he may enjoy eating. He gives enjoyment to man in eating food; man does not just simply eat. By enjoying food, we are nourished and our lives preserved. In like manner, God gives us a sexual urge that we may bear children, thus propagating the species. Whether it be the urge for food or the urge for sex, sin is not involved. Both of these were given in Genesis 2 before sin entered. We must be clear that this is God's view about these urges; they are good, for they were created by God.

2. LUST

What, then, is lust? When I am hungry, I may eat—and eat with pleasure; this is an urge for food, not a lust. But if I am hungry and have nothing to eat, and then think of stealing food from others, that is lust. Or if I eat indulgently; that also is lust. To think of eating is an urge; to steal to eat or to eat wantonly is lust.

We Christians eat when food is available. I often think that not only do we not steal or rob, we do not even think of stealing or robbing. This is according to the teaching of

Matthew 5. There is no lustful act, nor is there any lustful thought. When I see food, I like to eat; when I eat, I feel the food is tasty. This is the urge for food. It is created by God and has not a taint of sin in it. Where does sin come in then? It is when I have nothing to eat and think of stealing food. This is lust produced by the urge for food. By extending the urge for food into a desire to steal or rob, the urge has become a lust. In the Old Testament it says, "Thou shalt not steal" (Ex. 20:15). But in the New Testament a Christian who is hungry and has nothing to eat not only should not steal but also should not even think of stealing. Stealing is a lust, and so is thinking of stealing a lust.

The same applies to the urge for sex. As eating and drinking is to preserve individual life, so sex is to extend human life.

3. THE DEALING OF THE CROSS

Sex was originally good and so was eating. Both, though, may be turned into lust. Lust brings in extra demands and additional thoughts. The Lord Jesus has dealt with these already on the cross. He has crucified our flesh with its lusts and passions. This is indeed a glorious gospel. The cross has dealt with our passions and lusts. Consequently, no Christian needs to steal or think of stealing. We may be clean both in conduct and in thought.

4. THE POSITIVENESS OF GOD'S LIFE

This is not to say that we Christians do not deal with lusts and passions, but we do want to emphasize that the Lord has given us a new spirit and a new life. By this new spirit we may touch God, and by this new life we may manifest God's life. God's life is wholly positive; it is not negative. So it is not simply a matter of dealing with lusts; more is it a fact of positively touching the Spirit of God and manifesting the life of God. Only these positive things really satisfy us. For this reason, it is not for us Christians to lay stress on ordinances such as taste not, touch not, and handle not. Since we have the positive, we pay little attention to the negative things. We must help the brothers and sisters touch the positive and the glorious. Believers should always touch the glorious Spirit and the glorious life. Having touched these positive things, the things of taste not and handle not become very insignificant. It is good for Christians to be totally free of such earthly ordinances.

The people of the world do not have this positive outlook. If you take asceticism away from them, they have no religion at all. All they can do the whole day is stress these ordinances of taste not, touch not, and handle not. Take these away and you take away their world, for this is their world.

The Christian Life Is Flexible

The Bible provides quite a latitude on things such as food. Why is it that you may either eat or not eat? Because from God's viewpoint this is only a minor matter. God attaches no great importance to it. Instead, the Bible lays stress more on the positive. The life of the Son of God and Christ's life in us—these are the essentials, these are the matters of importance. Having that glory among us, eating and clothing become very minor indeed. This is why the Christian life, as shown in the Bible, is quite flexible.

If you wish to dress more moderately and eat less costly food, it is good. But if you have more money and feel like eating better or dressing in a more costly way, you may do it. In the same way, it is good if you decide today, for the Lord's sake, not to marry or be given in marriage. But, if you feel you do not treat yourself properly, it is equally right if you do get married. If one does not have the riches of Christ, to take marriage away from him would be to take his world away. But here is a person who does possess the riches of Christ; he can live with or without marriage. That which is positive is so great and glorious in him that he can treat these other things as insignificant. How big these problems are to a person measures how much Christ he has. Whether it be marriage or food, it is most insignificant in the Christian's life. The whole question turns on how much spiritual reality is manifested in our lives. If the glory of spiritual reality is fully manifested, other things will naturally fall into their proper places. But if the glory of Christ has not been obtained, these other things will loom large. Only those who do not know the Lord would attempt to deal with things through asceticism. For those who know the Lord, these things are easily solved.

1. EATING AND DRINKING NOT IMPORTANT

"But whereunto shall I liken this generation? It is like unto children sitting in the marketplace, who call unto their fellows and say, We piped unto you, and ye did not dance; we wailed, and ye did not mourn. For John came neither eating nor drinking, and they say, He hath a demon. The Son of man came eating and drinking, and they say, Behold, a gluttonous man and a winebibber, a friend of publicans and sinners! And wisdom is justified by her works" (Matt. 11:16–19). Here we see that the Lord Jesus Himself did not give rules for governing the external life of a Christian. He said that John did not come either eating or drinking, but He Himself came both eating and drinking. It is well to eat and to drink; it is equally well not to eat and to drink. These are not problems in themselves. John stayed in the wilderness; the Lord Jesus attended the wedding feast in Cana. Not eating or drinking, as seen in John, is Christianity; likewise, both eating and drinking, as seen in the Lord Jesus, is also Christianity. From the moment we possess the glory of Christ all these things lose their importance. May our thoughts, then, be changed so that we do not focus our attention on such things as eating and drinking as if these were real life. Remember, the reality of Christianity is neither in eating and drinking nor in not eating and drinking.

2. THE DISCIPLINE OF THE HOLY SPIRIT

"Not that I speak in respect of want: for I have learned, in whatsoever state I am, therein to be content. I know how to be abased, and I know also how to abound: in everything and in all things have I learned the secret both to be filled and to be hungry, both to abound and to be in want. I can do all things in him that strengtheneth me" (Phil. 4:11-13). Let us remember that a Christian is not necessarily filled or hungry; he knows how to be abased or how to abound. It is both to abound and to be in want. It is accepting the discipline of the Holy Spirit. It is well for me to go hungry if this is arranged by the Lord; it is also well for me to be filled if the Lord should so order. I am content to abound or to be in want as the Lord arranges. In other words, irrespective of what happens to me, the Lord will strengthen me with Himself. This is very positive.

I hope you will learn this flexible life before God. For a Christian, there is neither asceticism nor licentiousness. A Christian neither abstains nor indulges. His is a flexible life. His outward behavior is governed by the arrangement of the Holy Spirit, not by his own choice.

3. Transcendence, Not Abstinence

The word of Paul in 1 Corinthians 7 is very special: "But this I say, brethren, the time is shortened, that henceforth both those that have wives may be as though they had none; and those that weep, as though they wept not; and those that rejoice, as though they rejoiced not; and those that buy, as though they possessed not; and those that use the world, as not using it to the full: for the fashion of this world passeth away" (vv. 29–31). Such is a Christian. Since the Lord who dwells in him is so great, outside things no longer matter. For people to suppress these things or abstain from them merely proves how powerful these things are. Even those who most practice asceticism are sometimes the most filled with lusts and passions. Only he who is full of Christ is free from the problem of lust. He who has a wife may be as though he had none; he who has not a wife does not seek for one. He who weeps may be as though he wept not; he who rejoices, as though he rejoiced not. He may purchase things but as not possessing; use, but as not using the world to the full. The Christian transcends everything. His life is not abstinence but transcendence.

The Christian Standard Is to Be Maintained

Never entertain the erroneous concept that Christianity is ascetic in nature. Do not lower the standard of

Christianity and drag her into asceticism. The following stories illustrate this erroneous concept

1. SADHU SUNDAR SINGH

The famous Sadhu Sundar Singh was in Keswick for half a year. I was told that the family which entertained him was quite embarrassed. They prepared a bed for him, and the weather was rather chilly. But he slept every night on the floor. He was truly an Indian. I would hope, however, that we believers would learn to sleep anywhere, whether it is on a bed or on the floor, because this is Christianity. Some people have nothing within them. If they were to sleep on a bed, their Christianity would be gone! But let us be Christians whether we are to sleep on a bed, on the floor, or on the ground. Do not emphasize ordinances by turning the glorious, spiritual life into such things.

2. PREACHING AFTER ENGAGEMENT

A brother who was also a worker believed somewhat in asceticism. He was engaged one day to a sister. It so happened that the following day was the Lord's Day. Sometime afterward I met him and he told me a rather amusing thing. He said that he had felt very happy after he preached that Lord's Day because it had surprised him that he could still preach! Do you see his thought? He felt that he would not be able to preach because he had just been engaged the day before. He was considered as quite a good brother and yet he unconsciously accepted asceticism. Let us touch that which is glorious. Our Lord has already been raised from the dead and is now seated in heaven. If this light increases in us, other things will grow dim. Under the power of such a big life, all else will become very, very small.

3. LEAVING HIS WIFE AFTER MARRIAGE

An elderly pastor praised another pastor in Shantung, saying that he was so good that he had not seen his wife's face for two months after they were married. The day after he was married he left on a trip to preach the gospel. This is asceticism. If we read the Old Testament, we find that a man who was just married was not to go to war during his first year of marriage. The Bible takes special note of this date, for Christianity is not asceticism. The kingdom of God is not in eating and drinking. Whether we eat a little more or a little less is no problem at all, for God's kingdom is in demonstration of the power of the Holy Spirit.

4. NOT ABLE TO WORK

The first time two sisters were sent north of the Yangtze River to work, they wore overcoats. The Christians there doubted that any woman wearing an overcoat could do the work of God. They thought that God's truth is in the overcoat. If people wear overcoats, they cannot preach. But we know Christianity is not in an overcoat. It is most pitiful if people's Christianity rests upon an overcoat!

Christianity Transcends Everything

If Christianity were in eating, clothing, bedding, and so forth, how different would it be from the world? But today I can stand on the top of the mountain and declare that my Christianity is different from your dressing and your not dressing, from your eating and your not eating, from your joy and your weeping, from your using the world and your not using the things of the world. My Christianity transcends everything! The glorious life of God's Son, Jesus Christ, dwells in me. Daily I am being brought to heaven to touch the glory of the throne. This is Christianity.

Let me tell you, when that which is positive looms large in us, all other things will soon pass into oblivion. Do remember that a Christian is not an ascetic, but is one who lives a flexible life; for He who is in us is exceedingly great and glorious.

MANAGING YOUR FINANCES

After Selling All

In an earlier lesson we mentioned the matter of selling all in order to follow the Lord.* After one has responded to the call and given all, it is but natural that more money or wealth will again gradually come his way. How, then, should he manage it? To sell all is impossible with man but possible with God. To have the grip of wealth once loosened does not guarantee that it will not return. If a person is not careful, he may go back to the old habit of looking at his money as his own. A believer needs to learn continuously before God to give his money away.

The way Christians manage their finances is totally different from the way of unbelievers. The Christian way is to give, the unbelievers' way is to hoard. Our concern now is to know how a Christian should live on earth so that he may never be in want. Has not God promised us this? As the birds of the air have no lack of food or the lilies of the field of beautiful garments, so God's children should not lack anything. If they are in need, there must be a

* Volume 1, *A Living Sacrifice*, Lesson 3.

loophole somewhere. Those brothers who have a problem with income are usually those who have not managed their finances according to God's principle.

After you once sell your all and follow the Lord, you should henceforth hold to this principle throughout your life. You should manage your finances in God's way or else you will get into trouble. Many of God's children need to learn this lesson. We must learn how to live on the riches of God.

The Christian Principle of Financial Management

How should a Christian manage his finances? Read Luke 6:38. "Give, and it shall be given unto you; good measure, pressed down, shaken together, running over, shall they give into your bosom. For with what measure ye mete it shall be measured to you again."

As believers, we look to God for all our supplies. We live only through His mercy. The wealthy cannot depend on their wealth for food and clothing. During wartime, we have seen many rich people short in both of these. Paul exhorts us not to have our hope set on the uncertainty of riches nor be desirous of getting rich, for to do so will only pierce us with many sorrows (see 1 Tim. 6:7–10, 17–19). Only those who put their trust in the Lord, though they have no savings, shall not be in want. The Lord is well able to supply all their needs. But they do need to know that God's supply does have a condition attached to it.

If God is able to feed so many birds of the sky, He certainly can support us. No one but God could feed all the birds of the sky and nourish all the lilies of the field. He alone has the superabundance of riches to take care of the birds and the lilies as well as His own children. He would not have us be in such straitened circumstances that we can hardly live. Whoever has fallen into privation has not managed his finances according to God's principle. God has appointed a way for us to use our money. If we do not follow this law of spending, we will naturally fall into poverty. Only by following this law of God shall we be kept from want.

God is willing to supply our needs, superabundantly if need be. Never for a moment think that He is poor. The cattle upon a thousand hills are His; all things belong to Him. Why should God's children be poor? Why should they be in want? God is not one who cannot supply. He most assuredly can. But there is one thing we must do, that is, we must fulfill His condition before we are supplied. What, then, is His requirement?—give and it will be given to you.

I have seen some brothers in the midst of financial troubles. Their troubles, may I suggest, lie not in their inadequate income but rather in their insufficient giving. A basic principle the Lord shows us in the Bible is: give unto abundance but hoard unto poverty. The person who considers himself is certain to be poor, but he who gives is rich. God has spoken and it shall be done. In order to avoid poverty, you must give and give often. The more you give, the more God will give to you. If you are willing to give whatever is beyond your needs, one day you shall be given that which is beyond others' needs. Should you give one-twentieth to others, you will be given one-twentieth. If you give one-thousandth, you will be given one-thousandth.

If you give knowing that you will have no need because you have yet more stored away, who knows what will happen in the future? With whatever measure you mete to others, it shall be measured to you again. In the way you treat your brothers and sisters, God will treat you. If you give all your living to others, others will give all their living to you. But if you give what is useless t you, so shall others give to you. *Insufficient income is often caused by inadequate giving.* Proper giving almost guarantees a sufficient income. The Word of God is quite clear: "Give, and it shall be given unto you." You give to others, and the Lord will give to you. If you do not give, then the Lord is under no obligation to give to you. Many have faith to ask God for money but lack the faith to give it away. No wonder they often are destitute, even destitute of the faith to receive anything from God.

New believers ought to learn this basic lesson from the outset of their Christian lives. Otherwise they will not be able to go very far. Christians have a special way of managing their finances: give as you would like to be given. In other words, measure your income by giving. The world measures giving by its income, but we Christians measure income by giving. The measure we give will be that which we receive. Consequently, all who love money and bargain in giving are not able to receive God's money; they will not get God's supply.

We like to tell the brothers and sisters that everyone must look to God for the management of his or her needs. But, actually, God is pledged to supply only to one kind of person—those who are willing to give. The wording in Luke is indeed marvelous. It says, "good measure." When giving, God never calculates. He always gives bountifully. Our God is most generous; His cup always overflows. He is never stingy. He declares that He will give with good measure: "Pressed down, shaken together, running over."

Have you ever bought rice or wheat? Many sellers will pour the grain out of the measure without allowing you to shake it down. Not so with God. He will give with good measure, not only pressed down and shaken together but also running over. Truly our God is most liberal in giving. Listen, however, to what He says: "With what measure you mete it shall be measured to you." If your giving is calculating and exacting, then, when God moves people to supply your need, it will also be strictly calculated.

Two Pertinent Testimonies

1. MR. MOULE'S STORY

Handley C. G. Moule of England was the editor of *Life and Faith* magazine. Many things about him were highly commendable before the Lord. One of his strong points was his knowledge of the Bible. He lived by faith. Often he was financially tested, and just as often he was able to find out the cause of the trial, for he knew Luke 6:38. Whenever he was in want, he would always tell his wife that something must be wrong with their giving. He never considered how much they had given, only what was wrong with it.

Once, his food supply was reduced to almost nothing. Even the main staple of the English diet, flour, was completely exhausted. After waiting a day or two, nothing came in. So he and his wife prayed together, confessing their sin and acknowledging that there must be too many things in their house. Do you see, he did not ask the Lord first of all for flour. Rather, he told his wife that they must have too much in their house; therefore the Lord could not give. They knelt down and asked the Lord to show them wherein they had too much. After prayer, they searched their house starting from the attic, examining almost everything they had to see if there was anything too much. After going through every trunk, even through the children's clothing, they still could not find anything. Mr. Moule was then tempted to say, "Lord, we really have nothing too much. If You do not give, it will be Your fault." But after a while, he again said that the Lord could not be wrong. So, they continued their search until finally in the basement they discovered a case of butter given to them some days earlier. When Mr. Moule saw this case of butter he was very happy, for he knew this must be the thing in question.

At the time, they both were quite old and had learned the lesson of giving for many years. They knew the Word of God said, "Give, and it shall be given unto you." They cut the butter, wrapped the pieces in paper, and sent them to the poor among the saints. After they had finished giving out the butter, Mr. Moule said to his wife, "Now everything is clear." He knelt down and prayed, "Lord, I merely wish to remind You of what You have said: 'Give, and it shall be given unto you.' Please remember that we have no flour in our house."

This happened on a Saturday evening. Among those who received the gift of butter was a very poor sister, an invalid who was confined to bed. For many days she had had bread with no butter. So she prayed: "Lord, be gracious to me and give me some butter." Not long afterward, Mr. Moule came with a piece of butter. She thanked the Lord for answered prayer. A while later as she took her bread she prayed, "Though our brother is in lack of nothing, for he gives this butter to me, yet, if he should be in want, please, Lord, hear his prayer." Since Mr. Moule never allowed anyone to know of his lack, no one knew he was in need. Some even rumored that he was a rich brother. Did he not frequently give things to others? Had he not, in this instance, bought so much butter that there was extra for distribution? But this sister prayed for him. Within two or three hours, he received two bags of flour. His difficulty was over.

Let me tell you, we must believe every word of God. Many have difficulty with God's Word. They do not believe the Word of God as God's word. Mr. Moule, however, took God at His word. "Give, and it shall be given." May all new believers learn to give. Giving is not the end of everything; giving enables God to give to you. This is the Christian principle of managing finances.

If the giving is wrong, the receiving also will be wrong. If one desires to receive from others, then the principle is that the less he gets the more he gives. Then he will receive more. Many try to hold on to what they have in hand, so God permits them to have just that handful. They have not learned how to give. If the grace of giving is not in you, the grace of God will not be upon you. If you do not show grace to others, neither will God show grace to you.

2. MY FIRST LESSON IN GIVING

I have many testimonies concerning the matter of giving, but I will limit myself to just my first experience. It happened in 1923 when I was yet in school. I was invited by my schoolmate to preach the gospel in his city of Chien-Au, about one hundred eighty miles from Foochow. I asked my schoolmate how much the fare was for such a trip, and he figured it would cost me seventy or eighty dollars to go upstream by boat. The downstream trip would be somewhat less. So I said I would pray and see if the Lord wanted me to go.

At the moment I had nothing in hand. I prayed to the Lord, trusting that He would give the money if He wanted me to go. After prayer the Lord began to give, but when I counted the money it was still two or three times less than that required for the trip. I had only about twenty dollars and a little more than a hundred dimes. But my school-mate wrote and said everything was ready. He urged me to go immediately. So I cabled back the message that I would leave on a certain Friday.

On Thursday morning, the day before my departure, I was impressed by the word, "Give, and it shall be given unto you." I was a little troubled in my heart, not because I was unwilling to give all away, but because I could not possibly make the trip if the Lord did not further supply. Nevertheless, the impression within me grew stronger. I felt that I should give the dollars away and keep the dimes for my own use. To whom, then, should I give them? I had the thought of giving the dollars to a certain brother with a family. After I finished praying, I dared not say I was obedient; but neither would I say I was disobedient. I simply said, "Lord, I am here." I rose and went out, praying that I might meet that brother halfway down the road. Lo and behold, as I was halfway down the road, I saw the brother coming toward me. My heart sank, but I was ready too. I gave him the money saying, "Brother, the Lord wants me to put this money in your hands." Then I left. After walking away two steps, the tears rolled down my face and I said to myself, "I have already cabled my brother of my going there. Now the money is given away. Can I yet go?" On the other hand, though, I felt most peaceful in my heart, for had not the Lord promised, "Give, and it shall be given unto you"?

Now was the time the Lord ought to supply my need. But nothing came in on Thursday or on Friday. Another brother went with me to get the boat that took me to Hong San Bridge. From there I would take a small steamship to Swaykow. I was really frightened, for I had never left my native city of Foochow before. Since I had never been to the interior, I would not know anyone. After the brother sent me off, I prayed till I fell asleep in the boat. I said, "Lord, I have given to others; if You do not give to me, that is entirely up to You." On the very day that I arrived at Hong San Bridge, I changed for the steamship. I walked up and down the steamship several times, thinking that this would make it easier for God to supply my need. But I could not find any acquaintance on the steamship. Nevertheless, my heart still told me that since I had given, the Lord would give to me.

The steamship would arrive at Swaykow at four or five o'clock the next afternoon. From there I should again take a private boat for the last lap of the journey. This was the most expensive part and I had only a little over seventy dimes left. I was in a dilemma. I prayed this way, "Lord, I am now approaching Swaykow. Should I just give up the trip and buy a return ticket to Foochow?" But deep down within me there came a thought, "You are a fool. Why not ask God for a cheaper fare so you can go on?" I felt I had touched something full of meaning. So I prayed accordingly, "Lord, I do not ask You for money, but I do ask You to enable me to make the trip to Chien-Au." I had peace in my heart.

I was standing on the bow of the steamship. A boatman approached me, asking whether I was going to Nanping or

Chien-Au. I answered that I was going to Chien-Au. He said he would take me there for seventy dimes—less than what I had with me! As soon as I heard it, I knew the Lord had provided. I let him move my luggage to his boat. Since this part of the journey usually cost seventy or eighty dollars, I could not help but ask the boatman why his price was low. His answer was that his boat had been hired by the local government but that the official who occupied the front cabin had given him permission to take an extra passenger in the back cabin. Therefore, he actually was earning extra. I remember that I bought some vegetables and meat that day with the little money I still had. Thus I went to Chien-Au.

The trip back, however, was not any easier. I had only two dimes in my pocket. My school would soon open, so I had to rush back as soon as the meetings were over. I kept on praying. On the third day before my departure, I was invited by a missionary to have a meal with him. He said, "Mr. Nee, we have been greatly helped by your visit. Will you allow me to pay for your return trip?" Upon hearing this, I felt glad but also restrained. So I answered, "I already have One who is responsible for me." He asked my forgiveness for making such a request. When I returned to my room, I regretted what I had done. Once again I had spoiled the chance. But as I prayed, I had deep rest in my heart.

On the third day, the day of my departure, I still had only two dimes in my pocket. My luggage was sent forward to the boat and my schoolmate walked with me to the water front. I was praying all the time, "O Lord, You brought me to Chien-Au. Can You fail to take me back to Foochow? You are responsible for me, and You do not permit anyone else to take this responsibility. I am willing to acknowledge it if I was wrong, but I do not believe I was. The responsibility is Yours. You Yourself have said, 'Give, and it shall be given unto you.'" Midway to the boat, the missionary friend sent a letter to me by his servant. I opened it and read: "I know someone is responsible for you. But God has shown me that I should have a part in this visit of yours to Chien-Au. Will you allow an older brother to have a share? Please accept this little gift." As I received the money, I thanked the Lord saying, "O God, this money is right on time." In addition to using it to pay my return fare, I remember I spent the rest of it printing one issue of the *Revival* magazine.

After my return, I went to see my fellow-worker. His wife was at home. As soon as she saw me coming in, she said, "Mr. Nee, I want to talk with you. May I ask why you gave my husband twenty dollars before you left Foochow? Why did you put the money in his hand and immediately run away?" I said, "It was only that the Lord showed me, after a day of prayer, that I should give him the money. So when I met him on the road, I gave it to him." She answered, "Did you know that we had had the last meal and used the last fuel that same evening? With your money we were able to buy rice and fuel which lasted us until a few days ago when the Lord again sent in money. We had been waiting before the Lord for three days before we received that money from you." I did not tell her my story. But after I left her house, I mused on the way: If I had kept that twenty dollars in my pocket, it would have been dead, useless; but when it was given out, how useful it became. So I lifted up my head and told the Lord saying, "This is the first time I have really seen Luke

6." There and then I reconsecrated myself to the Lord. From then on, I would give; I would not leave any idle money in my hand.

It has been my hope that God would do miracles through my giving, that He would answer prayers through my sending out money. I will not retain any money in my hand, letting it stand idly. I dare not boast how experienced I have become in this matter. Perhaps I have given more and received more than the ordinary person. As a matter of fact, much money has passed through my hands. I speak as in foolishness. I prefer to send out my money that it may perform miracles and be answers to prayers; I do not want it to be idle and useless.

Young believers must learn how to manage their finances from the very beginning. I personally do not like to say too much, but I do want to testify to one thing. Since 1923 I have been down to my last penny many times, probably more than any brother in China. I know my own story and what the last penny means. But when I am in need, the Lord's word is: "Give, and it shall be given unto you." I learn today that as I give to others, God will supply my need. I know from experience that only those who give are those who receive. Time and again I have been shown that if I give liberally, the Lord will also give liberally to me. I would rather have the fame of "Brother Nee is rich." Yes indeed, I do have money, for I am always giving. But the return from it is manifold. Our God is never stingy.

The Christian Way of Managing Finances

The Christian way of financing is to not hold money tightly in hand. The tighter one holds on, the deadlier it becomes. Such money will be useless; it will melt away like ice. Only in giving is money increased. If God's children learn how to give, God will perform miracles everywhere. Holding on to money will reduce the children of God to poverty. Young believers must learn this lesson. They should not be content just to be saved; they must learn to experience the blessedness of giving. God cannot trust anyone who holds money tightly and does not give it out, for such a one is untrustworthy. The more one gives, the more God will give to him.

1. SOWING FOR GOD

"But this I say, He that soweth sparingly shall reap also sparingly; and he that soweth bountifully shall reap also bountifully" (2 Cor. 9:6). This Scripture also relates to the principle of Christian finances. Christians give money but they do not throw it away. It is not he who throws away that shall receive more; nor is it that he who throws away less shall receive less. What God says is that he who sows bountifully shall reap bountifully and also he who sows sparingly shall reap sparingly. Do you expect your money to grow? If you do, go and sow it. If you sow, the money will grow. Otherwise it will remain the same.

Brothers and sisters, can we be so foolish as to reap where we have not sown? Many prayers for supply are unanswered because we are hard men, reaping where we did not sow and gathering where we did not scatter. Why not take out a little money and sow it? Why not sow your money to many brothers and sisters who are in distress. Then you may reap afterward. He who holds his money tightly in his hand will not gain anything. Do you see the beautiful picture here? Paul says sending money out to help the poor—as the Corinthian believers sent forth to supply the needs of the saints in Jerusalem—is not throwing away but, rather, is sowing. Remember, money is like a seed which can be sown. If you meet brothers and sisters in distress and supply their needs, God will make that money grow until you reap thirty, sixty, a hundred-fold.

New brothers and sisters should learn to sow. Then when they are in need, they will reap what they have sown. You cannot reap what you did not sow. Many eat up all they have; naturally they have nothing left. Suppose you have a hundred pounds of grain and you sow half of it. The next year, then, you will have a harvest. And so on, year after year. Do not eat up all you have; leave some for sowing. Many Christians do nothing but eat; no wonder in the day of need, there is neither increase nor harvest. Let God send your money out to sow.

2. BRINGING TO GOD

God's Word concerning needs is very clear in the Old Testament. "Bring ye the whole tithe into the store-house, that there may be food in my house, and prove me now herewith, saith Jehovah of hosts, if I do not open you the windows of heaven, and pour you out a blessing, that there shall not be room enough to receive it" (Mal. 3:10), said God to the people of Israel. This gives the same principle we have just explained.

The people of Israel were in deep poverty. If they had tried to practice Malachi 3:10, they would probably have said that if their ten loads of rice were insufficient, how could nine loads possibly be sufficient; if their ten bags of flour were not enough, could nine bags be enough? Such foolish words are those spoken by natural men. God reproved the people of Israel by saying, "With men this is impossible, but with God all things are possible" (Matt.

19:26). "Bring ye the whole tithe into the store-house, . . . and prove me now herewith, . . . if I do not open you the windows of heaven, and pour you out a blessing, that there shall not be room enough to receive it."

May I tell you that ten loads is the reason for poverty while nine loads is the cause for abundance. One might reckon that the more he has in hand the better his financial condition. But such a one does not know that this is the basic reason for his poverty. If we bring to God, we enter into blessing; if we retain in our hand, we will be cursed. The extra load we bring to God's storehouse will become our blessing; if we withhold it, it will be our curse and even the other nine loads will be swallowed up. In keeping back that which belongs to God, we shall see poverty.

3. SCATTERING FOR GOD

"There is that scattereth, and increaseth yet more; and there is that withholdeth more than is meet, but it tendeth only to want" (Prov. 11:24). Many do not scatter, so they have nothing left. But they who scatter become rich before God. This too is shown us by God's Word.

4. SPENDING FOR GOD

There is another wonderful event of which we may take note. When Elijah prayed for rain, the nation was suffering under a great drought. Both the king and his chief chamberlain were out searching for water. Such a scarcity of water can easily be understood. But when Elijah offered a sacrifice and prayed for rain, he ordered them to pour water on the burnt-offering. How very precious water was at that time, yet Elijah made them pour water three times on the sacrifice till the water ran

211

round about the altar and filled the trench. Considering the fact that rain from heaven had not yet descended, was it not a pity to pour away so much water? What if the rain did not come? But Elijah commanded them to pour out the water. He knelt down and prayed that God would send fire to consume the offering on the altar. God heard that prayer and also his prayer for rain; He sent down a great rain. Let me tell you, if you want heaven to send down a great rain, you must first pour on your water. If you spare the water, you will not get the water from heaven.

Here lies the problem of many. They hold on tightly to what is their own and yet expect God to hear their prayers. God is ready to call off the drought, but He waits for men to pour on the water. The human thought is always to have a way of retreat ready. In case rain does not fall, there are at least twelve jars of water. But those who count the jars of water at hand will never see the water from heaven. Whoever wishes to have the water from heaven must be willing, like Elijah, to spend the water at hand. Let everything be spent, not only the cattle and the sheep but also the water in hand. The same principle applies to the matter of money. Unless new believers are delivered from the power of mammon, the way of the church can never be straight. May we all be consecrated people who lay our all on the altar for God.

5. SUPPLIED FROM GOD

"And my God shall supply every need of yours according to his riches in glory in Christ Jesus" (Phil. 4:19). This indeed is a marvelous verse. The Corinthian believers were tight in giving, but the Philippian believers were generous. Time and again, the Philippians had sent supply to the apostle Paul. Paul, in turn, answered them that his God would supply all *their* needs according to His riches in glory in Christ Jesus. Do you see the wonder of the verse? Paul especially mentioned "my God," that is, the God of the one who received the supply, for had not the Philippians sent money to Paul? "My God shall supply"—He would supply those who had supplied Paul. It was the God of the recipient of the gift supplying the needs of the givers of the gift.

Many today try to lay hold of Philippians 4:19. Do we, though, see in this verse that God shall supply the givers, not the askers? Only the givers have the right to use this verse; those who do not give are not entitled to the privilege. After giving to others, you may say, "O God, supply today all my needs according to the riches in Christ." God supplied all the needs of only the Philippians. God supplies on the principle of giving.

When your jar is nearly empty of meal and your cruse of oil, remember first to make a little cake for Elijah the prophet of God. Then your handful of meal and few drops of oil will last you for three years and six months. Who has ever heard of a cruse of oil that lasted three and a half years? But if you use a little meal and a tiny bit of oil to first make a cake for God's prophet, you shall be fed for years. That handful of meal and those drops of oil are not enough for one meal; nevertheless, if first given to God, they may sustain you for life. Such is the way Christians manage their finances.

The Christian Way Is in Giving

Both the Old and New Testaments lay down the same teaching. God does not want us to be poor or in distress. If there is poverty and distress among us, it may be that we have held our money too tightly. The more we love ourselves, the more we will be hungry. If the money question is not solved, nothing is solved. To whomever money looms big, the threat of poverty is near. I may not be able to testify to other things, but to this I can testify; the tighter one holds on to money, the poorer he becomes. May we release our money and allow it to be in circulation doing miracles for God.

The cattle on a thousand hills and the sheep on ten thousand hills all belong to God. Who but a fool would think he must earn them? All we need to do is to bring our all to God. We should send money out as soon as it comes in. We should take care of brothers and sisters in need. To hoard for ourselves is foolishness. The way of a Christian lies in giving. Let all the money in the church be living money. Then when you are in need, God will perform miracles, even sending the birds of the air to supply you.

Put yourselves into the Word of God, or else God has no way to perform His Word in you. First give yourselves to God, and then release your money that God may give to you.

TITLES YOU
WILL WANT TO HAVE

By Watchman Nee

Basic Lesson Series
Volume 1 – A Living Sacrifice
Volume 2 – The Good Confession
Volume 3 – Assembling Together
Volume 4- Not I, But Christ
Volume 5 – Do All to the Glory of God
Volume 6 – Love One Another

The Church and the Work
Volume 1 – Assembly Life
Volume 2 – Rethinking the Work
Volume 3 – Church Affairs
Revive Thy Work
The Word of the Cross
The Communion of the Holy Spirit
The Finest of the Wheat – Volume 1
The Finest of the Wheat – Volume 2
Take Heed
Worship God
Interpreting Matthew
The Character of God's Workman
Gleanings in the Fields of Boaz
The Spirit of the Gospel
The life That Wins
From Glory to Glory
The Spirit of Judgment
From Faith to Faith
Back to the Cross
The Lord My Portion
Aids to "Revelation"
Grace for Grace
The Better Covenant
A Balanced Christian Life
The Mystery of Creation

The Messenger of the Cross
Full of Grace and Truth – Volume 1
Full of Grace and Truth – Volume 2
The Spirit of Wisdom and Revelation
Whom Shall I Send?
The Testimony of God
The Salvation of the Soul
The King and the Kingdom of Heaven
The Body of Christ: A Reality
Let Us Pray
God's Plan and the Overcomers
The Glory of His Life
"Come, Lord Jesus"
Practical Issues of This Life
Gospel Dialogue
God's Work
Ye Search the Scriptures
The Prayer Ministry of the Church
Christ the Sum of All Spiritual Things
Spiritual Knowledge
The Latent Power of the Soul
The Ministry of God's Word
Spiritual Reality or Obsession
The Spiritual Man
The Release of The Spirit
Spiritual Authority

By Stephen Kaung

Discipled to Christ
The Splendor of His Ways
Seeing the Lord's End in Job
The Songs of Degrees
Meditations on Fifteen Psalms

ORDER FROM:

Christian Fellowship Publishers, Inc.
11515 Allecingie Parkway
Richmond, Virginia 23235